RCIA and You

Practical Experiences and Ideas for Leaders

Blessie La Scola

RESOURCE PUBLICATIONS, INC.

Resource Publications
Distributed by Liturgy Training Publications, 3949 South Racine Avenue, Chicago IL 60609, 1-800-933-1800; fax 1-800-933-7094; email orders@ltp.org. See our website at www.LTP.org.

Library of Congress Control Number: 2014942041

ISBN: 978-0-89390-776-1

Printed in the United States of America.

L 20 19 18 17 16   2 3 4 5 6

Design and Production: Patty Sweet
Cover Illustration: Virginia Silvers
Copyeditors: Barbara Mellen and Caroline Thomas

DEDICATION

This book is dedicated to my husband and best friend, Ernie. It is in thanksgiving that I offer my deep appreciation for his continued support, encouragement, gentleness, and patience for the passion that we share for the RCIA process. It is his love for God and his faith that continues to be a great example for so many others and me. My heart is deeply and forever grateful.

APPRECIATION

I thank all those who have given encouragement and been examples of the converted heart for my life of faith: my parents John and Helen Akers, Fr. Larry Largente, Fr. Bernie Brannon S.J., Fr. Robert Fabing S.J., Rev. George Collins PhD., Ruth Spencer, Patrick and Virginia Silvers, Jim and Fran Bermudes, Joseph Stallings, O.S.U., Fr. Christopher Bennett, Blessed Mother Teresa, St. Francis of Assisi, my children, their spouses, my grandchildren, and my husband. I also thank all those team members who have dedicated hours to welcoming and sharing with those seeking love.

CONTENTS

FOREWORD

Dear Reader:

To be human is to search for God. Throughout history down to the present moment human beings have given expression to their search for God in religious beliefs and practices. God gives us minds to search for the truth and hearts that long for unconditional, forgiving love. These basic human desires are fulfilled in God who is truth and love, and take us on a great journey.

Blessie La Scola has a wonderful gift of helping us to look at the journey. *RCIA and You* is an enthusiastic celebration of many journeys of the RCIA process, especially a process of conversion through the sacramental life of the church.

It also has a unique way of connecting our story to that of Jesus the great teacher, calling us to reach out for God's best for our lives. It is rich in its use of the Word of God, balances the different aspects of a person's journey to baptism, and provides a real stimulus to parish life.

In *RCIA and You*, Blessie helps us to see that the Rite of Christian Initiation of Adults is the fruit of a renewal of the catechumenate of the church in the first centuries. This was the way in which adults who came to the church seeking faith were gradually helped to respond to the Gospel and to prepare to be baptized and connected to the story of Jesus.

In the pages that follow, Blessie helps us focus on the specific roles and responsibilities for conversion and sacramental formation within the parish especially relating to the pastor, parish staff members, and other consultative bodies. By applying talents and dedication to the RCIA experience of parish life and spirituality, all who exercise leadership and service in the parish contribute to a welcoming journey.

The Gospel according to Matthew closes with Christ's final words to us, *"Go, therefore, and make disciples of all nations, baptizing them in the name of the Father, and of the Son, and of the holy Spirit, teaching them to observe all that I have commanded you."* (Mt 28:19-20) This book is intended to help RCIA teams do just that.

I invite you, dear reader, to take time with this book. Appreciate the journey which it asks you to travel. This book should prove an inspiration to many who share together the journey of RCIA.

Fr. Christopher Bennett
Pastor, Santa Teresa of Avila Parish
San Jose, California

Introduction:

Why I Wrote this Book

On November 11, 1986, the *Rite of Christian Initiation of Adults* was canonically approved by the National Conference of Catholic Bishops. The Apostolic See subsequently confirmed it by decree of the Congregation for Divine Worship on February 19, 1987. Then on July 1, 1988 the *Rite of Christian Initiation of Adults* was allowed to be published and used in liturgy. On September 1, 1988 it became mandatory in the dioceses of the United States of America to use the published rite and no other English version. Consequently we have been using this rite for fifty years and we are still challenged to understand its meaning for the church.

The *Rite of Christian Initiation of Adults* is a document that provides an opportunity for evangelization and conversion. I never thought, as a catechist, that the rite was *only* for sacramental initiation; I believe it is for sacramental living. Therefore, I never saw the RCIA process as a form of sacramental preparation. I see it as a process of conversion where one journeys through receiving the sacraments of initiation to live a sacramental life for and with the church. This perspective came to me while attending the institute called Beginnings and Beyond given by the former North American Forum on the Catechumenate. I was able to attend five different institutes by the Forum, each offering a deeper understanding into the rites of Christian initiation of adults. Some of the institutes were about those who were unbaptized; others about the candidates, those already baptized who were in the process; some were about the children in the process, and still another about the dismissal rite. I continue to rely on the information and formation I received while attending these institutes to provide understanding of the rites, the process of the rite, and the theological background for the process.

This book is a result of the experience I had in serving others in the process, with some materials and activities that worked and some that did not. In these chapters you will find my opinions, things tried that worked with the specific group of people attending, stories that made a difference in how we shared the faith, some creative ideas, and my own journey within an evolving process. *This is not a commentary to the rite.* However, you will find many parts of the rite referred to or quoted because I work closely in relationship with the rite and its commentaries. This book attempts to offer experiential ideas for an adult ongoing process, and for a process that includes children and youth. I hope my experience is helpful to those just starting to learn or beginning to serve in the process with adults, youth, and children. I have always been thankful when other catechists shared their ideas with me, and I hope to share what I have learned through experience.

This is not a book that provides lesson plans for you, lists of what to do, or defined activities. This book encourages you to trust your creativity, your faith story and experiences with Christ in your own life, and how you celebrate the sacramental life today. In the RCIA process we are asked to first welcome the people who come to us, to listen to their story, and then to plan from their spiritual needs what we will address in each session. This is not a school plan—it is a conversion plan. The main drive for us is to introduce those who come, whatever age, to Christ. As their meetings with Christ continue through sessions with us, they come to a time when they are ready to announce their hearts' conversion. It doesn't matter how many years or sessions it takes, or how old they are when they receive the sacraments. What matters is that they are developing a strong and powerful relationship with Christ, one that will last and carry them through whatever life brings later. We want them to be celebrating a sacramental life as they grow.

I also wrote this book because I am an advocate for God's children, of all ages, to come to know Christ in relationship and sacrament. We cannot be too young or too old. We are never too late. When people call to ask about the process it is because the Holy Spirit tapped on a shoulder, pushed them to sign up, sent a flyer, played a song, or through a relative spoke words that triggered an action. People enter the process at the precise time that God intends for them to enter. We are the church, ready to welcome at any time whomever God sends to us. Nurturing their relationship with Christ is our first and foremost function. How we do that is what the process is about. The model is doing what Jesus did. It sounds easy and simple, but we do have challenges, as we are perfectly human; so flexibility and openness of heart and mind are very important in this ministry.

This book includes ideas that I welcome you to take for your own use. Many of the stories are real-life stories from my experiences with those journeying in the process. As you meet others on the journey you also will have stories. Each one is important because it is about the change in a person's life. It is their story joining our story, and our stories connected to Jesus' story, that makes this spiritual journey so powerful in life. How can any of us go unchanged? I hope this book challenges, causes questions to arise, encourages further reading, creates more questions, and deepens your own desire to walk the journey in a new way.

CHAPTER ONE:

A JOURNEY IN FAITH

My passion in ministry has been the rite of Christian initiation process in the Roman Catholic Church. It has been a growing experience of understanding my faith and developing a relationship with God. I have always been part of the Christian religion; however, there was a period when I was challenged in my personal faith journey. I had no idea at the time what the challenge really meant for my life. I had been raised in the American Baptist tradition and was quite content. My faith was strong and I felt called to continue serving God as I began college. During my years of elementary schooling I had friends who were Catholic, but I never ventured into any discussion. It was in high school when I first heard from one friend that she was not allowed to even enter my church since she was Catholic. This didn't make any sense to me. Then later I was invited to a dance at the Catholic Church where the same friend attended. It was fun and the priest in charge seemed accepting enough. Little did I know that the Divine was already laying ground for my future.

I met my future husband in college and discovered that he was Catholic. I still remember his shocked face when he finally came to understand that my father was one of those protestant preachers. We were married in 1967 after attending a Pre-Cana Conference for couples seeking to be married in the Catholic Church. The Pre-Cana Conference was very helpful and I enjoyed all that I learned and appreciated the support of those in leadership. At this time we also met with a priest, who just happened to be the same priest I had met at the dance in high school. He provided further understanding of the theology, answered questions, and gave guidance for our future as a couple. I was never asked to change my belief system, to leave my faith tradition, or to denounce any of my faith. I was asked to raise our children in the Catholic tradition. I had no objection to this since Catholicism is part of the Christian religion.

By 1972, my husband and I were proud parents of two children, busy with work and school. During this time I began to ask deeper life questions that were developing within me. We had been married for seven years and I began to question further the differences of our two faith traditions. I found some books and decided to read in private so as not to stir up any expectations. My husband and I had always been respectful of the other's faith tradition; he didn't ask me to change and I didn't ask him.

It was two more years before my heart could embrace fully the teachings of the Catholic Church. It ended up being nine years into our marriage before my initiation into the faith. So whenever someone asks me about entering the process I always think of the length of time it took me. I have had time to reflect and ask myself about how much time I needed and why. Consequently, I believe it is never in the best interest of a person's faith journey to have them meet another's agenda of time.

In 1983 my husband and I were asked to lead a pilot program for children and youth who were children of the adults in the RCIA process of our parish at the time. It was our first experience with the RCIA or catechumenate model; we were trained catechists and yet we limped our way along. Our first group was composed of ten young people, and the book we were given to use was far beyond what they could understand, so we gave up the book and began to put together a different curriculum based on what they needed to understand and eventually own. We wrote down the many questions they asked, read over their answers to the reflection sheets we gave out, and listened to them intently when discussion took place. With this information we were able to build a curriculum. As the years began to bring more children and youth we took the training available by attending the North American Forum Institute for the Catechumenate. Our first change was our own attitude toward catechesis. We needed some structure to our sessions, and for two years we had witnessed what it takes to introduce Jesus and an understanding of Catholic Christianity to another person. It was not giving out books to each person to carry back and forth to sessions; nor was it in testing for results in comprehension. It was in allowing *time* for each person to enter and get to know each other and the process at their own pace. We needed to introduce topics, challenge them, pray, play, share in activities, break open in discussion groups, and listen to each one. The openness allowed each person to find his or her own path to come to know and follow Jesus.

Whether serving the adults, children, or youth in this process, the rites offer insight into what the curriculum needs to offer. It was during the children's track at one institute that I understood how to look ahead to the rite to be celebrated and find some of the subject matter ahead of time to prepare for discussion. For example: when we look to the rite of acceptance in the *Rite of Christian Initiation of Adults*, paragraph 41-43, we find what is expected for someone participating in the rite. This gives catechists some understanding of what is necessary before the precatechumenate participants move forward to the rite of acceptance and/or rite of welcome.

CHAPTER TWO

THE IMPORTANCE OF *TIME* FOR RELIGIOUS FORMATION

I have three vital questions to ask parents who are in a hurry for their children to receive the sacraments:

1. How long do you want your child to be Catholic and do you want them practicing their faith later in life?

2. Whom do you want your child to call on when troubled if you are not present?

3. Has your child expressed any desire or interest in coming to the sacraments of the church?

Another three questions to ask adults entering the process:

1. What brings you here at this time in your life?

2. What makes this important for you right now?

3. Are you interested in being Catholic all your life and practicing the faith? Why?

When asking questions to parents, most will answer, "Yes, we want our child(ren) to practice their faith and we pray they will call on God at all times."

It is necessary to work with the expectations of the parents. There will be some who answer differently; however, working with parents' expectations is necessary in this process of bringing the children and youth to the faith. This is a process that offers a well-rounded faith to all children and youth. If nourished and practiced for as long as it takes for them to fully desire the sacraments, then quite possibly the grown child will practice their faith and be strong in it. If the child is hurried, and the church simply administers the sacraments due to the parents' or catechist's agenda, then we may question whether the faith is strong enough to last when needed in the grown child's life. There are thousands of Catholics who attend church on a regular basis, but does this mean they are faithful? What are their reasons for attending? Is it out of habit, fear, doing what is right, or practicing what they were taught? How many have, in their lifetime, come to share in a relationship with Jesus Christ? It is this relationship with Jesus Christ that is to bring us together to celebrate as the larger family of God. Allowing time for that relationship to develop in the process gives the possibility of a sustained faith.

When I shared with the parents that the "class" would possibly be two or more years, they were baffled. Needless to say, many of the parents didn't like to hear this at first. They wanted a definite—and shorter—time period, something they could write on their calendar. We, the church, need to hold a different attitude than what society begs of us. We are to be the ones passing on the living Word of God, the Good News. Do we care how this is delivered and received? Are we truly offering the best we can? Have we, the catechists, given time to our own formation in the process? Opening the *Rite of Christian Initiation of Adults* text is the best way to discover, and to be enlightened to a deeper understanding of what we need to bring to those who are on this journey of faith.

I would like to refer here to areas of the *Rite of Christian Initiation of Adults* document, the RCIA book. First, to #18 located in the "National Statutes for the Catechumenate," found in the back of the rite book. This statute offers the basis for why the children follow the same pattern of formation as the adults in this process. Then turn to paragraph #75 of the *Rite of Christian Initiation of Adults*. There we find expectations of what we as catechists are to offer during the period of the catechumenate. Paragraph #75.1 mentions "a suitable catechesis" and then proceeds to explain to us what that means. Do take time to read and reflect on these areas for your own journey in faith.

Paragraph #75.2 offers further elements of what catechists bring to those in the process. In case you feel overwhelmed or alone in this endeavor, continue reading paragraph #75.3 and find that the community is to be supportive through liturgical rites and prayer. The community is to participate in this process. We do not do this alone. We are to call upon community members to help in the many areas of the process.

If parents need help in understanding the process, then we, the catechists, need to assist them. We can share with them the passage from the *Rite of Christian Initiation of Adults*, paragraph #253:

> The Christian initiation of these children requires both a conversion that is personal and somewhat developed, in proportion to their age, and the assistance of the education they need. The process of initiation thus must be adapted both to their spiritual progress, that is, to the children's growth in faith, and to the catechetical instruction they receive. Accordingly, as with adults, their initiation is to be extended over several years, if need be, before they receive the sacraments.

It is our job as catechists to help parents, children, and youth come to an acceptance of allowing God's time to work with them. We are to be the example of this in our own lives.

The parents are invited to follow our lead. Sometimes they will try to maneuver things to go their way, but if we are strong in our own understanding of the need for time in the process, then they will feel secure and come around in their thinking. It is a matter of building trust with the parents, children, and youth.

I began building a process by looking at my own understanding of unlimited time. Then I took this understanding to the team members who would be working with the participants. Others involved would be the priests and the community, each asking and sharing in discussion of what unlimited time means when people are being brought into the faith. What are the expectations of the leaders and community as far the readiness of the one embracing the faith? The initiation process is open to all ages, seven to seniors. Each person deserves the time to be given the best. Sometimes they need to be guided to slow down so they have time to let the process work.

This, of course, is not our usual way of thinking. We usually structure catechesis or religious education as an academic form, following a planned calendar with specific topics. This structure is used in order to offer content to give the participant the understanding and knowledge necessary for either the sacraments or a grade. This may or may not lead the participants to form a personal relationship with Christ. The idea of offering more time is foreign to us since we have had experience for so long with a structured form and a specific amount of time for learning. It has been either grade-level classes in a school environment, or grade-level classes outside of the weekly school schedule, but still held in schoolrooms with the same structure. For adults, the academic content has usually been offered through a series of lectures.

It seems that many children, now grown, remember how they were taught by memorization and testing. Where does the personal relationship with Christ enter into this? As a person grows to adulthood, he/she may find that personal relationship and growth in faith continues. No one will argue that just because one learns by rote they cannot have a relationship with God. The position of the church is to form their faith to lead them to Christ, to form and open their hearts and minds to Christ's love and forgiveness. I believe that beginning earlier is better! The content that children learn by rote can touch their hearts if they are led to relate it to their personal experiences in life.

There is the challenge of messiness in the process. The process is not neat and tidy. If we really have the process going all year long with people coming in at all times of the year, it is hard to keep track of who is where and who has learned what. Lots of questions arise as to how one can manage such a messy process. We tend to like clean finished lines. Years ago I was given a plaque, which I hung next to my desk: "Let's organize this thing—and take all the fun out of it!" This is what we want to do—organize the process according to what we want, (without taking all the fun out, of course), but we can't. People and their lives are messy. The church is made up of people; in fact it is the largest dysfunctional family there is! We keep trying to clean up the mess and then some more comes in! Life is messy so we must as team, directors, leaders understand that the Spirit is the driving force behind a person entering the church, and trust in the Spirit's movement within the person's heart and mind. This does not mean that we do nothing to organize. There is much we can organize: contact information, sacramental needs, sponsor and participatory forms, and planning. Little by little during the process, much of this is done during the time you have together. By the time the person proclaims their readiness, you are also ready.

Encouraging the staff, the community, and the team to understand and accept the unlimited amount of time needed in the process for those participating is another challenge. If we, as the leaders/directors/coordinators of the process, can change our attitude about time being unlimited, then others will follow. As the attitude of those around us changes, the participants will feel at ease as well, and know there is no rush. They will sense the freedom of being able to learn and develop their relationship with Jesus, come to a secure and grounded understanding of the church teachings, and discern in prayer their call to service. We as Catholics are so excited to find a person journeying towards the sacraments, to once again feel their anticipation and witness their enlightenment, that we tend to hasten their journey rather than be relaxed in where they are. It is hard to be a listener without offering more information for them right away, even when they are not ready to receive more.

In the Gospel of Luke 7:1-10, we find the healing of the centurion's slave. I have often wondered how long the centurion waited before encountering Jesus. Was it days or months? What was it that prompted him to go outside his own people, cross over the boundary and enter into trusting another way of believing?

Also in Luke 18:18-23 we find a rich official who approaches Jesus and wants to know what else he needs to do to "inherit eternal life." How long had he been thinking of this? He knew all the commandments and had followed them well. Why couldn't he go any farther in his transformation? What made him go another way? What was he holding on to? What was holding on to him?

Notice that Jesus in both accounts allows the person to approach him. Jesus welcomes and listens. Then Jesus offers either a question or a challenge of action for their journey in faith. It will take different amounts of time for both. The centurion is already making movements in his life for change and proclaims out loud his faith in Jesus' actions for healing. The rich young man is still tied up in his material belongings; his wealth is in the way of him being free to hand over his life to follow. He is still owned by material and personal goods and unable to change or proclaim his faith. Maybe more time is needed?

A gentleman and his wife entered our process. He met with our pastor, and because of his background in theology, being a minister in another Christian denomination, I was told that he would be a candidate for the second period of the process, the catechumenate. It was already planned that he would receive his sacraments that very Easter. The month was October. I did question and offer my objections, but it had already been decided. So, when given lemons, make lemonade, right? It wasn't that this man did not have faith in God; it was that his faith was from a very fundamental form of interpretation. The team was put to the test during those months. None of us have forgotten how we challenged him, and sometimes ended up in the pastor's office. When I look back I can see how this man could have used a process that allowed more time. During Easter that year he was welcomed into the Catholic Church. One year later I received a card wishing me happy Easter. He and his wife were serving at a protestant church. We have had an ongoing relationship through the years, and I know he and his family returned to the Catholic Church. It is only because of the Holy Spirit, and that this man's heart was open to Christ, that he is serving in the Catholic Church today. I feel that we have such richness in our Catholic Church that most people are not ready to receive it too fast; they need time to consume and digest.

Chapter Three:

Why Process Instead of Program?

In our faith formation programs we do hand over or pass on information from our history and tradition within the Catholic Church. However, it is not handed on as data, but as building blocks for a foundation of faith in one's relationship with Christ and the church. The significant difference in programs is that usually they all begin and end at a specific time, then repeat what was offered as they begin again. Most people who are considering entering one of these programs must enter at a given time in order to benefit from the information offered, and usually the information is required before passing on to another grade or level of information. Most people who want any formation in their faith attend a class from September to May. This is not considered an ongoing process.

The *Rite of Christian Initiation of Adults* process lends itself to having people enter at *any* time of the year, literally the whole year. However the majority of processes I have come in contact with, for adults or children, are usually open for nine or ten months, with a break for summer.

A general misunderstanding is the meaning of process. One definition is the steps it takes to put together or manufacture an object or those steps taken to accomplish a task. We can understand a process to also mean that which takes time, as in evolution or life maturation. All people mature at different levels as well as different speeds, and with different outcomes; life in all aspects evolves, with time being the common denominator, each form of life taking the time necessary to become what is needed for the universe.

A process for growth in the Spirit is similar. It needs time to be able to spread out, to be comfortable and trust, to ask questions as questions come, to take a step back when necessary, to gain an understanding of the consequences of actions taken in the process and outside the process, to grow in knowledge of the faith and in relationship with Christ and his church. The Christian initiation process is created to give the necessary time for each person, no matter their age, to come to an experience of initial conversion, and ultimately conversion of their heart to Christ. This needs time that is given in a process instead of a limited program.

Most who enter this process, and sometimes those already baptized in the Catholic tradition, come in without having experienced what they would call an initial conversion. They come seeking something— many times something they are unable to put into words; they just know that they feel alone, empty, lost, or that they need something in their lives that seems to be missing. There are some who come with an already developed knowledge of their Christian faith. They experience an active relationship with Christ in prayer, and they are ready to deepen their understanding of this relationship with Christ as relates to the church's teachings. Each of these people deserves the best process that can be offered, which means the timeline may be different for each person in the process. Each person deserves to be responded to with a "custom made" process.

One of the most helpful articles ever written on the subject was by Ron Oakham, called "Sorting Fish". It helps a director or coordinator in placing a person into the process and in developing an appreciation for the time needed in the process.

If we can let go of calendars, agendas, or expectations that the participants will finish on time for Easter sacraments, then maybe we can begin to offer the faith-growing process that will truly bring one to a deeper relationship with Christ. As the participant's relationship deepens, the church will become their companion during and after their journey in the process. As companion, the church will teach, encourage, pray, celebrate, guide, and give counsel for their continued growth in love of Jesus Christ. Those participating will watch and learn from the full church.

There have been religious programs called RCIA, offered to specific ages, that meet from September to June, incorporating a once- or twice-a-month session for adults, children, or youth. The reasons differ from one parish to another as to why they choose this format.

- Not many people are participating or have this specific need.

- The team is too small to handle the number of participants and their needs.

- The director or coordinator may be holding two or more positions in the parish, and a nine-month program may be the only way to offer sessions at the time.

- The priests may find it difficult to support this as an ongoing process for the adults, children, and/or youth.

To hold a formal process in a church requires one person who can build a team from the community to serve the needs of all who come searching. If the director or coordinator is holding two or more positions, one of them being the RCIA leader without a team, then they will not have the time needed. No one person can do all this. The process suffers and so do the participants.

In speaking with many directors who have had two or more positions along with the RCIA, many of them could not remember each story or name of the individual participants. How sad to think that a person is coming, trusting, opening themselves up to someone in the church who will not remember their name, the story of their journey, or maybe what group they are in for receiving the sacraments. If a director is in charge of the overall catechetical department, there can be an overwhelming number of people. There are different processes for the needs of individuals. There are those in sacramental preparation or restored order for children seven years old, and maybe those who are a bit older. Then there are those needing only confirmation in the middle school or high school age. There may be an adult confirmation group, and then the RCIA for adults or children. How can one person truly offer the best of themselves to all these people? Whether very few or many participants, a team is always better for all involved.

CHAPTER FOUR:

HOW DOES A PROCESS FOR ADULTS, CHILDREN, AND YOUTH WORK?

Children from the age of seven to seventeen are welcome into this process, as well as adults, age eighteen and older. However, in the various parishes I have observed there seem to be questions and doubts about serving children in this process. I have not found many leaders and catechists who embrace the idea that children from the ages of seven to seventeen are able to experience an "initial conversion." We, the leaders and catechists, have doubts about the child's or youth's ability to understand all we think is necessary, and instead limit their experience in the process to having an acceptable knowledge of church teachings and the sacraments.

As a result, this runs the risk of not offering the child or youth a full experience in relationship with Christ as a formation in the faith—only information about Christ. We have the opportunity to give information *about* Christ and to offer time for developing a relationship *with* Christ through experiences in one's life.

Whether the children and youth attend the parochial system and religion is part of their everyday curriculum, or they attend the different catechetical formation programs of the parishes, all catechesis is and should be first about the building of the child's relationship with Christ. If we ignore the everyday lived experience of God in the development of religious formation for the children and youth, then all they receive is information about a building where a group of people gather in the name of an unseen and unknown source. If, in fact, we do have a relationship with God, then it is no longer the building or how we gather that becomes most important; it is that the temple of the body, of the person, is part of the larger Body of Christ that is important. Then a want or a need to be present can develop, and we offer ourselves in faithful action to participate *in* community.

It took our team about three years for the adult process to accommodate the full year-around process; and it happened naturally, as some inquirers chose not to move forward to the second period. They discerned in prayer that they needed more time in the precatechumenate period. At that time we were offering the rite of welcome and/or rite of acceptance into the order of catechumens once a year. When these inquirers chose to continue in the precatechumenate, things changed. We began to offer these first rites three times throughout the year, during an ordinary season of the liturgical year.

The *Rite of Christian Initiation for Adults*, #44, states, "The rite will take place on specified days during the year (see no. 18) that are suited to local conditions."

From Thomas Morris' book, *The RCIA: Transforming the Church*, in chapter five we read, "The rite, which is celebrated at various times during the year depending on need, consists of various parts … (p. 70)."

We find in Nick Wagner's book, *The Way of Faith: A Field Guide for the RCIA Process*, chapter 10 (pages 47-48), "The Rite of Acceptance can take place on almost any Sunday of the year. Some Sundays, however, are better than others. … Ideally, a parish would choose two to four possible Sundays on which to celebrate the Rite of Acceptance in the coming year."

In all of these statements it is understood that it is natural to offer the rite of acceptance more than once a year, if we are allowing time for the formation of faith. This means that not all participants move forward at the same time, nor at the same time of year.

At first we tried to bring the same transition to the children's process. What we found out was that, because of the many family situations, not all children were as available to attend during the summer as the adults. There were shared custody issues as well as vacations. Also, we discovered, we really needed to promote family. This meant it was necessary to put our teaching into personal practice, meaning to value our own families and take time with them. Of course we did not come to this understanding right away. We planned outdoor events, crafts, prayer, games, picnics, you name it, but if the people were not in town how could they attend? Families take vacations too!

We continued to try for two summers before we determined we were not paying attention to the facts in front of us. So, how does a process for children become year-around, if the children and youth are "let out" for the summer? This was the question and challenge.

We decided to accept children and youth into the precatechumenate period at any time during the school year. This meant that even after Easter was celebrated, when some parents realized that their children were not baptized, they could call and receive a welcome. We would sit down and let them, the family, all enter into the process, the precatechumenate period, with the understanding that they would attend the sessions until the end of May and then continue after the summer break in September. If a family called in February, we would sit and hold an interview or conversation with them, register the child into the first period, and they would attend until May. In September, the next season, they would continue that period. This way the first period of precatechumenate became ongoing, accepting participants all year, bringing them in whenever they called. This meant that messiness had entered the process. Paperwork becomes very important in this change. Someone must keep organized paperwork.

Again, it was Ron Oakham's article "Sorting Fish," which helped us pay attention to the individual stories of each adult, child, and youth. The children or youth entering were a mixture just as in the adult process, some baptized and some not. Questions arose as to where their baptisms took place, or whether they needed a longer precatechumenate than another entering at the same time.

We found in twenty-five years of serving in this process that all adults, children, youth, and parents are not the same. Almost all who enter come with some experience or knowledge of God in their lives (maybe they just aren't aware of it), and those few who come with some formal teaching in their background usually need updating and an experience of community. This does not mean that we plop everyone into a "one size fits all" process. The church has done that for too many years! We are so used to accommodating our needs instead of accommodating those we are called to serve. We tend to look at the numbers and are overwhelmed at the time we will spend in paperwork and choose to "clean up" the program. We tell ourselves that they will get what they need. This may be true, but will it be the best for their relationship in and with Christ? And is it the best we can give?

Finding the proper placement for each adult, child, or youth in the process requires time. This requires a person who will sit with them and their families, ask questions and listen, find out about the family—where they come from, and what the person has already experienced in faith. When this takes place, a better understanding of which period the person is ready for becomes apparent.

Our first and foremost valuable resource is the *Rite of Christian Initiation of Adults*. Again, #253 states, "Accordingly, as with adults, their initiation is to be extended over several years, if need be, before they receive the sacraments." This statement gives credibility that the process works best when given the time necessary. Each person needs time to develop their relationship with Christ, and to come to an *initial conversion* leading to *full transformation* in their faith.

As we began accepting children and youth into the process at any time of the year, it meant that the second period, catechumenate, must be ready for those children and youth who were ready to move through the first rites. This meant another team. My husband and I could not do all this ourselves; we needed help. We chose to begin meeting on a weeknight with the precatechumenate families, and on Sunday morning with those in the catechumenate or second period. Teams were developed using people who had been helping us in the precatechumenate, and who now moved on with those who were ready.

During this slow process we developed a form of curriculum. Many resources were presented to us for use. We never chose to buy any of these texts for each child or youth to use in the process. Occasionally we did purchase one for our own resource, but we always found if we went by the limited curriculum in the text we were not following the first and most important aspect of the process—to offer unlimited time for initial conversion to take place, and to develop the curriculum from the stories, questions, issues, etc., of those before us. In the years of our service a style of curriculum did develop, only because of the many questions and needs expressed by the participants and what we learned. However, we did not think that what we had planned for any session was more important than what they brought or needed to discuss at that session. Believe me, we have often spent over an hour with children or youth sharing and debating the answers to questions they brought to sessions!

It was a Sunday family gathering for the children in the catechumenate period. We had a full house, meaning a large number of children enrolled, about 20, which meant there were 35 to 40 people in the room with parents and sponsors attending. When all had signed in and we had prayed, it was the custom to ask for questions. Elizabeth raised her hand. That day she was with her grandparents, who were serving as her godparents in the process. Elizabeth was small for a fourth grader, one of those young girls with the inner wisdom of an old woman. She could come up with the most profound statements at the most unexpected times. This was one of those moments. She said that the question she had was a hard one; that I might not be able to answer it and I might have research to do. I accepted the mission and invited the question. Her question was, "Who exactly came first? Was it Mary or Jesus?" You could have heard a feather float by, the room was so quiet. Not even an adult hand went up to answer; they just all stared at me. What I realized in that finite moment was the awesome power of God working in the heart and mind of this young girl. She was truly in touch with the mystery of God by asking this question. I have never heard a more profound question than this one, even from an adult. This question led, of course, to a discussion of the Trinity, the core of our faith. The discussion was lively and wonderful, full of energy and everyone learned, all because of a question from a fourth grader.

In my view, the structure of an RCIA—or any other process—is built upon hospitality, welcoming, acceptance, listening, teaching, challenging, sharing, praying, community, and sending. If all these elements are within every session, then the model of the catechumenate is present. If, however, teaching outweighs sharing and listening, then it is not this model. First the participants' needs are to be expressed and heard. Let's look at the order of these elements in relationship with the model, knowing that none of this takes place overnight.

1. We offer openness to another person at the door or where they enter, hospitality with the "Hello, please join us," name tags so that all can become known by name, a cup of beverage, a comfortable place to sit, a friendly and inviting environment that makes a person want to be there, and a genuine presence of ourselves. This does not mean a fancy decorated room is needed for hospitality. It means that the room and attitude of those welcoming need to be inviting.

2. As all are gathered, there is a formal welcome that includes mentioning the joy we all feel in having these new participants join us. This is about the importance of them being with us, and the difference it already makes in our lives that they have come.

3. As the gathering continues, acceptance of each other's presence will naturally take place; not in one session,

but over weeks. A trust in each other and of the place we are in can build, bringing ease within the group.

4. It is in listening to each participant's story, shared in pieces over weeks and sometimes months, that we begin to become part of each other's story. The worries, doubts, troubles, questions, struggles, joys, and heartaches that are shared by all during the sessions build layers of trust so that one day the heart opens and is ready to receive the teaching of the church.

5. Hearing and absorbing the teachings of the church offers each person another perspective on life; a new way of seeing is opened to each person involved. All present receive a gift in hearing God's word and how the church has responded through the ages.

6. The teaching brings with it challenges for all our lives; for change, for looking more closely at how we make decisions, how we have related to others, and in what direction we are going next.

7. It is in these challenging times that people open up to sharing and a flood of hope comes pouring out in emotions around the circle. The emotions can be negative sounding or positive. Either way it is growth that is taking place within each person because we are struggling with our own truths and the truth that Jesus is calling us to.

8. Prayer is obviously part of the entire process; however, it is now that we find the participants in deeper prayer than they even thought possible. They are coming to a place of need, a need for Jesus in the flesh.

9. Jesus in the flesh is found in community. The participants find a need for the community around them including those they do not know but who have been supporting them with prayer and encouragement all along.

10. The time of initiation is the formal moment when they are sent out into the world to share the good news. Time for discernment is given to recognize Christ's call and to walk in whatever direction that he is asking.

This structure is the same one Jesus used with his own disciples. With Peter, he first caught Peter's eye, probably struck up some easy conversation, and then invited Peter to follow him. There was an immediate acceptance within Peter's heart as well as in that of his brother. They were already interested; they had been waiting for someone like Jesus for a while. Jesus listened to them, he taught them of the Father in a way they had never known, challenged the norms of the faith by which they were living, shared in debate and conversation, prayed, brought them to see the importance of community, and sent them forth to do the same. This took three years. The only difference in this structure is that Jesus did not put any time limit on growth for each disciple. He just kept listening, teaching, sharing, and praying. His expectations were different from ours. Even though he had little time, he still continued at their pace. Everyone grows at a different speed and we need to be open to allow children as well as adults to grow in the faith at their own speed, not ours.

Chapter Five:

Process Is Important

Before working with the catechumenate, my husband and I were teaching a class of sixth graders in our home, following the curriculum of a text on Hebrew Scripture. The children began discussing the leaders of the church at that time and the word pope was mentioned. One of the students was new to the area. He had been baptized as an infant and had already received his first Eucharist at the normal age of seven. He asked the very first question, one that established the baseline from where we would later form a curriculum. He asked, "What is a pope." Of course all laughed, not realizing that he was serious; however it opened up a very good discussion and my husband and I have never forgotten it.

Three years later we began working with the children whose parents were in the adult catechumenate. We were not yet officially part of the process; but we met with them once a week for a year and introduced the faith to them. They had so many questions we felt we had only begun to touch the surface. The next year the children were mainstreamed into the grade level classes for regular catechism.

Our second year we offered the same introductions to the faith, only we chose to use what we had learned the previous year and used the Bible as our main resource and text for all. This was better, but we felt we could offer more if given the proper training. That was when I attended the Beginnings and Beyond Institute with the North American Forum. It was there that the model became more apparent for me, as the *structure of the process and of the rites* was explained. When I returned, we asked the parish to allow us to have the children meet for at least two years: The first year for the introduction to the faith, and the second year to offer the preparation needed to receive the sacraments if the children were ready.

After a lot of discussion we were given permission for the process with the children to begin. This helped create the inquiry year or precatechumenate for beginners, and it worked. I know that other parishes have entered these children and youth in sessions with others their age who are already baptized and who have previous formation in the faith. I have heard of some positive experiences, however we kept doing what we were doing and our numbers grew.

There were still challenges for the children taking part in the rites with the adults. The challenges were the scrutinies, celebrating the Easter Vigil with the adults, baptizing the children by immersion, days of reflection or retreats, and whether confirming a child as young as eight or nine is beneficial. At the time the sacrament of confirmation was only for high school age participants or adults. One foundational challenge for the team and the community was accepting one process for all ages.

Before I was asked to take the position of Director of the Catechumenate, the RCIA for the adults and children had never been seen as one process. This was my first task. Once again it was the institute and the use of the rite book that gave me understanding into working with all the different needs and ages. First I had to help the parish staff and team see the process as one. Then we started within the community as announcements were made, events celebrated, and explanations offered by word of mouth. Everyone has to use the same vocabulary, hold the same vision, and trust in each other. This all takes time. We never got it perfect, but we kept trying and doing our best.

Parents liked having a space where they and their children could ask any question that came to mind; it was the beginning of building trust. The parents no longer felt alone because they had not had their child baptized as an infant; there were other parents just like them. This was also a way to bring the families into the church, not only for formation in the faith, but literally to bring them into becoming members of the body. A community would begin to form among them as they shared time with each other in the sessions as well as at Mass. Consequently, our inquiry for children began to grow from 15 children to 25 and then to 35 each year. When you have 35 participants, each bringing one or two parents, you can have quite a crowded place. However, we always seemed to have room.

We developed the youth and child process to be intermingled, meaning ages seven through high school were combined into one setting. Our reason at first was that there were two of us and only ten of them so we just started together to see what would happen. It was awkward at first, teens wanting to know why they were in a group with younger children and the younger children being a little intimidated by the older ones. However it took only about two sessions before we were all chumming up. What happened? In addition to lots of ice breakers, everyone realized that they could ask any question, and everybody else wanted to know the answer too. They were no longer in a place where they were afraid to ask about whether God had a mother and what was her name, or if Jesus knew he had a stepfather and how did he feel about it. Everyone was on the same level when it came to wanting to know about Jesus and this faith of ours. Once that was established, we were ready to learn together!

Besides being free to ask questions, the mixed ages attending looked like what we see in church. When we go to church and are sitting in the pews, people of different ages are all around us. We all come to listen and take part, to learn and to pray together. Our session came to be a smaller model of that church setting. We all came together to learn, to listen, to pray, and to grow as one body. What happened while we were not watching is that the high school boy was suddenly joking around with the younger boys, the older girl was helping the younger girls, and they all began to pair up in odd matches that God brought together. It was quite inspiring.

Every other week we had what we called a family gathering, which meant that one or both parents, and the sponsor (during the catechumenate period), were expected to attend with the child or youth. The reason for parental participation is usually assumed to be only for the benefit of the children and youth, but that was not our only reason. The parents needed to learn and to pray with their children and youth. They needed to participate with them in the practice of the faith in a safe space in order to take it home and practice every day. The other reason was to build communication between parent and child or youth about the faith and issues in life. We hoped to stimulate interest in asking more questions and discussions on the way back home after the session.

One other aspect to our sessions for the children and youth in both areas was that of faith-work. This is not homework; it is faith-work. Yes, they did take it home. The work had to do with their thoughts and attitudes about issues or topics in life in relation to the teachings of Christ and the church. It was through the faith-work that the children and youth offered personal insights and gave their ideas and solutions to challenges or events. This offered us catechists the spiritual information we needed to assess their growth in faith. We did not grade these; but we all took turns taking them home to read over, and wrote comments back to the child or youth on their ideas and answers. Once in a while we sent home something called parent faith-work. The children and youth were always happy about this because they knew that their parents would have work to do. It was to stimulate within the parent some of their own faith story to share with their child or youth along the way, or to bring them some insight to their growth in faith. From offering this for the parents we were blessed to have many attend the adult process a year or two later for their own preparation for the sacraments.

CHAPTER SIX:

WHAT MAKES THE PRECATECHUMENATE PERIOD IMPORTANT?

It is important to respect each period of the process of Christian initiation. In so doing we respect the individuals, their relationship with Christ, and their journey. In our first meeting with someone, it is easy to think to ourselves that this person is very knowledgeable, has just been away for a while, that they can catch up easily, or that they need only some updating. We forget to offer the proper amount of time for each person to spend in the process. We forget that there are many areas of a person's life that may need to be examined with respect to their relationship with self, Christ, and the church. If the amount of time in the various periods is limited by curriculum or anticipation of the sacraments, the faith growth of an individual can be shortened and many times stopped.

Think of the people who sit in the pews at church during Mass. What do they remember being taught about their faith? Why do they attend church? What is their relationship with Christ like, and is it different than when they were a child or youth? We have had many experiences of youth and adults who come to the process with the understanding of their faith of a seven-year-old child, or whenever they last celebrated a sacrament. They were not given the opportunity, or it became unimportant to them for a time, to develop their faith as they aged. We need deeper insight into the individuals who come. By listening to their statements and their times of sharing, we begin to know what in their life needs growth in the love and forgiveness of Christ.

The first period, precatechumenate, is for evangelization. Evangelization is more than hospitality and being friendly. Webster's gives the definition as "a zealous effort to spread the gospel." We ask ourselves: In what way was Jesus a zealous evangelizer? What kind of evangelization did St. Paul go through as his life changed? In Scripture, neither Jesus nor Paul indicate that the experience is just about feeling good; each is about facing truth and coming to recognize the will of God in their lives. This is true for us as well.

To quote from the *Rite of Christian Initiation of Adults*, part one under the "Outline for Christian Initiation of Adults," the period of evangelization and precatechumenate "is a time, of no fixed duration or structure, for inquiry and introduction to Gospel values, an opportunity for the beginnings of faith (page 14)."

The period of evangelization is without a fixed time or structure, where gospel values are introduced and the opportunity is given for faith to begin. So it becomes important to find out from those attending how their relationship with God, Father/Jesus/Holy Spirit, is. This gives the catechist a direction to go. What have they experienced of the gospel values? Are they familiar with the Bible, Jesus' teachings, the church's response about living in the world and this society? Are they facing issues in their lives that do not reflect gospel values or Jesus' teachings? It is during this period that a person is challenged to a personal and spiritual change. Understand, we are not the ones who make the decisions for those attending; they make their own decisions. However, if we do not give them the knowledge or understanding they need to make a decision that may require change, then we are the ones who are to blame. Are we about giving strength to the new Catholics, or do we only want them to like us? Do we hesitate to rock the boat? Do we anticipate them leading a life of faith or not? We are the teachers, those setting the example. It should be made clear what we as Catholics expect so they understand the direction in which they are journeying. This may sound heavy-handed, but it is not intended to be. We are called to echo the faith with love and trust.

A list of topics was developed from our years of listening to those participating. As the years passed we found ourselves using the topics on that list, in addition to topics the participants' brought up during their reflections and formational discussions. Each group of participants surfaced needs to learn or know more about certain topics, so each time we used the topics in a different order based on the needs of the group. At the end of each session we would introduce the next session, which would be based on some of their questions, issues discussed, or needs stated. Consequently, the list is still in use today. It is basic and only for the first period, that of the precatechumenate.

What is faith?
Our faith story
Our search for God
Faith and trust
Belonging
Revelation of God
Jesus' story
The human Jesus

Call to change
Holy Week
Easter
Resurrection
Tour of the church
Our Mass
The Bible
Old Covenant; Abraham, Moses

The divine Jesus	New Covenant
Prayer; kinds, styles	Parables and teachings of Jesus
Lent	Creation stories
Sin	Mary
Forgiveness	Church and community
Advent	Christmas

As mentioned before, we offer the rite of welcome for the candidates and the rite of acceptance into the order of catechumens three times during the year. We also celebrate the rites combined. This means good preparation is very important, not only for the participants, but also for all involved. It became clear to me during my second year that the participants needed more understanding of the rites than one informational sheet or session. The rites of welcome and acceptance call for deeper awareness by the individuals into the meaning of living out a gospel way of life and the cross of Jesus. Three transitional sessions were developed for those who determined they were ready to move forward to the rites. At a precatechumenate session, one of the team introduces the upcoming preparation to those present. The participants know how long they have been attending the sessions and if they are ready to move forward. If they determine they are ready, they are invited to sign up that evening and receive a phone call during the following week to let them know where they will meet. It is scheduled on the same night of the week and at the same time as the current sessions, but in a different space. During these times it becomes necessary for the adult teams to split and be available for the three areas of the adult process. Usually one of the catechumenate team members and one from the precatechumenate team come together for these transitional sessions.

The first session in preparation for the rite is an

introduction to the catechumenate period. We offer this to help the participants feel comfortable with the different periods of the process in which they are journeying, and to offer some reflection and discernment. What is this period about and what does it require and expect of them? It is designed to include Scripture readings and reflection, a beginning of discernment regarding the process offered for their prayer, and a reflection booklet to work on individually. This can be taken home and returned if they do not finish it during the session. Use of the booklet helps a person discern his or her readiness to move forward or not. One was put together for the children and youth and one for the adults. Both were found to be useful. The one for the children and youth was more to their level of understanding, but did ask and require the same reflection. We adapted the content of the reflection booklet from the *Rite of Christian Initiation of Adults* paragraph #42, and from Thomas Morris' book, *The RCIA: Transforming the Church* under the chapter on the "Rite of Acceptance into the Order of Catechumens." For the adults' discernment we were able to create questions that reflect the areas of readiness described in Morris's book. For the children and youth we were able to be creative in our presentation using clip art, questions, and statements to be finished by them to gain the information we needed. Both booklets offered space for participants to state their readiness according to their own feelings. If after reflecting and completing the booklet they stated they were ready to move forward, then two more sessions were offered in preparation for the rite. If they discerned that they were not ready, they were invited to continue in the precatechumenate period for as long as was necessary for them.

If a child, youth, or an adult states with real honesty that they are not ready to move forward, what do we do? It was a learning moment for the team, the staff, and me when this happened the first time. Our first experience was with an adult who had journeyed for a year and two months in the precatechumenate. At first we all felt that maybe we had not done our job well. That was not his reason. When I read his booklet with his statement, I truly questioned why he did not feel ready. So, I called him and asked if we could meet. He had been pretty regular in attendance, but had missed a number of weeks during the Lenten season. He felt that this had left a "hole" in his understanding of the story that he needed filled. I explained that he would probably receive all that he needed the next year, but he refused my reasoning and decided to continue his journey in the precatechumenate even though it would be longer. He was in no hurry. WOW! He continued for another year and six months before receiving the sacraments of initiation. This meant that he journeyed for nearly three years in the process. Today he is active in our parish and when I see him I know he was right. I am so thankful that I listened.

In the 1990's we noticed that in working with the children and youth it had become almost a common practice for about one-third of the group to choose to *not* move forward the first time around. It was a natural response for many who had come with little or no previous faith formation. They enjoyed the simplicity of the precatechumenate year and needed more time for their faith formation. Usually during the second time around they were attending Mass as a family. This helped them begin to connect what they were experiencing at Mass with the teachings from the sessions. Each time there was a child or youth that felt they were not ready to move forward, we would meet and offer time for them to convey the reasons for their decision. One or both parents would be present to listen as well; however, it was made clear to the parents that the child or youth was the primary decision-maker in this process. Many times I would leave the parent and child/youth together in my office so they could discuss if the child's decision was appropriate. Usually the parent would come to an acceptance of what their child decided.

The second session in preparation for the rite of acceptance into the order of catechumens was on "The Gospel as a Way of Life" and the third session was "The Cross." These two sessions were sometimes held together as a day of reflection, a mini retreat. Bringing the two topics together, the gospel and the cross, was quite challenging but meaningful. In working with the adults, some of the team preferred the day of reflection so as not to have any separation between the two topics. They felt the impact was greater when all was presented as one. Others preferred the more casual weeknight sessions, where each session could focus on its own message to challenge them. Either approach had an impact and touched the lives of those preparing for the rites.

In working with the children and youth we offered them a day of reflection, bringing the two messages together as one. One of the favorite activities we offered is that of searching for one's own cross. We had different kinds of crosses hanging around a room with their titles and information. Each cross represented a saint or an event in church or biblical history. The children and youth were allowed to roam for a time and find the one cross that seemed to call to them. They had a form to fill out asking which they chose and why. In sharing later with the children or youth, much was revealed about themselves in their understanding of suffering and of Jesus. The follow-up activity to this was to create their own crosses with different materials. Our favorite was an old design using clothespins to build a crucifix. The children and youth would glue the pieces of the clothespins together to form a cross; then the corpus would be formed, also from clothespins. They all took them home to hang on their walls. One year the team made one for the group to have during our sessions. At the end of the day together we had each child and team member sign his or her first name on the cross as part of the closing prayer. This cross was placed on the prayer table for our sessions and became a focus throughout the year together.

Having these three transition sessions came to be a part of the process for us. It seems odd to think they were not part of the process when we first began, but as in many things, we too had to evolve. Now they are a natural part of the process. They give the team members an opportunity to really see each person's stance in the process. They are also of great help to those participants in the group who need further clarification for their journey. The formation that "The Gospel as a way of Life" can offer is abundant and to stand under the cross is an overwhelming experience for anyone. Each of us needs to take account of our way of life relative to the gospel and where we stand in relationship to the cross. The time given to those who are new to the journey offers those of us too comfortable in our journey a chance to take another look.

The question is: How can anyone publicly proclaim their faith for the first time in front of community, if they have not been given knowledge or understanding of what they are proclaiming? If the Bible is not introduced or given to the inquirer, how will they come to know the word of God? If the teachings of Jesus are not offered or introduced, then how are the inquirers to know how to live by them? If the cross of salvation, freedom, resurrection, glory, victory, is not spoken of, then how can it be known? If we believe that this process is to be unlimited in time, then it is with great passion that we should bow to God's time in bringing the faith to others.

Those who enter the process already baptized are to be challenged just as much as those who come seeking baptism. They might be people who have been attending church since they were seven years old or younger, and who now come to complete their initiation with confirmation and Eucharist. Whether we place them into the RCIA process or not, we must ask questions and listen. Have they been faithful to practicing their faith through the years? What are their needs in their faith formation? There are many questions during a first conversation or interview that help in learning what the individual needs during this time of evangelization. As catechists, we also must make notes about their questions and sharing during this period of evangelization. We find that the catechesis offered to the candidates (those already baptized) needs to be different from that offered to the catechumens (unbaptized). This requires enough team members to break out into separate groups for discussion during the sessions.

One year a man came to see me about being part of the team. We sat and talked and I found out that he had just been fully initiated in another parish of the diocese. He was full of that early excitement and passion to serve others as he had been served. I, too, was excited to have such a person on the team. It was at the end of our meeting that he stated he had a few questions. One was, "could he have a Bible and would I teach him how to read it," and two was "what was the prayer with the beads; he was interested in learning that." My response to him was to reach for one of the extra Bibles in my office and sit with him for a few more minutes to open it together and then allow him to take it home. I also went to my file and took out information on the rosary that I gave him along with a set of simple rosary beads. It took only a few more minutes and he was so happy to have this information. When he left I sat in silence, in prayer for all those who have come to our church hungry for the word and love of Christ. How many have been sent out with great faith, but maybe without some of the essentials for continued nourishment of their faith? Although we were already using the New American Bible as our text for the sessions in RCIA, this affirmed for me why we were doing so. It also made me question what kind of catechesis this gentleman had had in preparation for his rite of acceptance. I wondered if accepting the gospel as a way of life and the cross was part of his formation.

We form many individuals in the faith throughout the years, but sometimes we forget to allow time for evangelization. To allow time for the heart to be moved, for the mind and behavior to change, is what evangelization requires. We can all be educated and learn the information needed to be part of a group or community. But, if we are to make the necessary changes in the way we live our lives so that the love of Jesus can make a difference in us, then the catechesis and time given should reflect this.

CHAPTER SEVEN

THE CATECHUMENATE PERIOD

Those who are seeking baptism enter this period by the celebration of the rite of acceptance into the order of catechumens. Speaking in a pure sense, this period is for only the unbaptized. However the majority of us in parishes have found ourselves including in this period those who are baptized but who have had no previous catechesis. Many of us combine the rite of welcoming for the candidates with the rite of acceptance. In the *Rite of Christian Initiation of Adults* it is included as a possibility, although not encouraged, but made possible for the situation. Paragraph #506 states "In the catechesis of the community and in the celebration of these rites, care must be taken to maintain the distinction between the catechumens and the baptized candidates". This is not a sentence to take lightly, but to pay close attention to.

It is the parish priests, the director of the catechumenate, catechists, and other leaders in the process who are in a position to guide those who are foreign to this process and its language. We are held accountable for how we interpret the rite, so we must make certain of the credibility of our statements and guidance offered. When we are forming another in the faith even a small thing to us like a word in vocabulary can make a big difference in the growth of their faith and understanding. If we give credence to the rites then we need to spend time reading and understanding them. The community depends on us to make clear for them who is who (baptized, unbaptized, candidates and catechumens), and what they are doing and celebrating. When a catechumen or candidate doesn't know the difference in their titles for their faith journey, then you can be sure their sponsor doesn't know either. Whose fault is that? It is ours. We, the leaders, are the individuals who need to spend enough time with each part of the process to see that each person has what he or she needs for their journey. We are helping them to pack for their journey. If something important is left out, the journey will be off track for a time. There are always glitches in the process, and people are people. However our job is to know the process well enough that we can be present for their journey to give the guidance and support they need. If, by the beginning of this second period, there are questions or doubts as to who is who in the group, take care of it. Do it before the rites are celebrated so that each can hear the words with understanding to take to heart and mind.

All of the following are to be discerned in some manner with the individual, their sponsor, and possibly a team member. It is suggested and encouraged that the pastor or priest involved in the process also be present. Before celebrating the rite of acceptance into the order of catechumens and/or the rite of welcome for the candidates there are some prerequisites. The following list of prerequisites is taken from paragraph #42 in *Rite of Christian Initiation of Adults*:

Beginnings of the spiritual life
Fundamentals of Christian teaching have taken root
First faith conceived
Initial conversion and intention to change their lives and
    to enter into relationship with God in Christ
First stirrings of repentance
Calling upon God in prayer
A sense of the church

Experience of the spirit of Christians through contact
     with the community, priests

We also added:

Acceptance of living the gospel message
Acceptance of the cross

These topics come from looking ahead to the rites and are part
of the instruction suggested in preparation for the liturgical
rite.

Once the rites have been celebrated and the catechumens
and candidates are formally within the second period, there
are many topics that need to be discussed. This is a time for
definite and clear catechesis. However we need to remember
again that we have years, if needed, to offer any curriculum.
The outline of the process states that this period can be for
more than one year. We do not have to hurry nor are we the
only "teachers" these people will ever have. We have been
given specific material to work from and the lives of each of
the individuals present. By now, we will have spent enough
time with them to know what their personal needs are as far
as church teachings and reflection for further transformation
of heart and mind. If we have not spent enough time with
them and do not know them, then we will depend upon only
written material that we asked them to return to us. It is of
utmost importance to get to know them personally.

As I listed some topics for the precatechumenate period,
I also have a list of some of the topics we covered during the
second period. You will notice that some of the topics are
repeated due to people entering the second period at different
times of the year.

Bible—Old and
New Covenant

People of the Bible

God's divine revelation

Prayer as our response to God

Reconciliation/sacrament of
anointing

Sacraments of service

The humanity and divinity of
Jesus

Sin and temptation

Our Creed, Nicene

Saints of the church

The Trinity

Advent, the liturgical year

The incarnation

Christian decision making,
morality

The Mass, history and parts

History of the church

Baptism

Confirmation

Eucharist

Discipleship

Lent

Social justice

Conversion of the heart

Our thirst

Our blindness

Our tombs

Holy Week and Passover

Triduum

Resurrection

Being missioned to serve

Pentecost

Mary, model for the church

As you can see from reading the topics, many take a few weeks to cover. I will say that our meetings were never boring or dull. We always had a lot of discussion. I guess one question would be how to arrange these topics. We placed them according to the gospel reading for the Sunday before. That way we were able to continue to break open the gospel during the session with adults and children and then move directly into the subject. This flowed well. Also, there were numerous times, and I mean many, when we entered a session with adults, children, or youth and found ourselves talking about something totally different from the topic. The discussion then centered on what was necessary for those present, where they were in life, in their faith journey, and in the present moment.

What could be more important than that? Nothing. When the Iraq war began, we had many children whose relatives were affected by this event. Two of our sessions in one month were about war. We looked into the Old Testament, the New Testament, and the *Catechism of the Catholic Church* for research, and we prayed. What took place during those two sessions will never be forgotten; they were some of the best because it was where all our hearts were.

One other aspect of the entire process, but especially for this second period, is time for self-reflection. We built into each session a certain amount of time for individual reflection, then small group sharing, and finally a coming together with the larger group. We found this format to work most times with just about any age. The questions or statements for reflection were kept general to the topic, but included the participants' feelings, actions they might take, or their suggestions for change. On occasion we had only individual reflection questions that were more personal. When we brought the group together, those who felt comfortable sharing would do so. When we did not have time built in for individual reflection, we would send home a sheet with reflection questions for them to spend time with and bring back. The purpose was that of deeper conversion, not a psychological study of self. We talk about reaching the heart of the person in this journey, although we know that we cannot do this without reaching the mind as well. But in this journey of faith it is the heart that must do the most work. The mind can remember all kinds of data, hold knowledge of what is correct and right, but it is the heart of the person that will dictate their actions the majority of time. There is a very old story called "A Parable" that can bring this to light. I have no idea who wrote it, but I was introduced to it during my own training to become a catechist.

1. *I took a little child's hand in mine. He and I were to walk together for a while. I was to lead him to the Father. It was a task that overcame me, so awful was the responsibility. And so I talked to the child only of the Father. I painted the sternness of His face were the child to do something to displease Him. I spoke of the child's goodness as something that would appease the Father's wrath. We walked under the tall trees. I said that the Father had the power to send them crashing down, struck by His thunderbolt. We walked in the sunshine. I told him of the greatness of the Father, who made the burning, blazing sun. And one twilight we met the Father. The child hid behind me. He was afraid. He would not look up at the face so loving. He remembered my picture. He would not take the Father's hand. I was between the child and the Father. I wondered. I had been so conscientious, so serious.*

2. *I took a little child's hand in mine. I was to lead him to the Father. I felt burdened with the multiplicity of the things I had to teach him. We did not ramble; we hastened from spot to spot. At one moment we compared the leaves of the different trees. In the next we examined a bird's nest. While the child was questioning me about it, I hurried him away to chase a butterfly. Did he chance to fall asleep I wakened him, lest he should miss something I wished him to see. We spoke of the Father, O yes, often and rapidly. I poured into his ears all the stories he ought to know, but we were following a brook, which we must trace to its source. And then, in the twilight we met the Father. The child merely glanced at Him and then his gaze was not interested enough to stop. He dropped exhausted to the ground and fell asleep. Again I*

was between the child and the Father. I wondered. I had taught him so many things.

3. *I took a little child's hand to lead him to the Father. My heart was full of gratitude for the glad privilege. We walked slowly. I suited my steps to the steps of the child. We spoke of the things the child noticed. Sometimes we picked the Father's flowers and stroked their petals and loved their bright colors. Sometimes it was one of the Father's birds. We watched it build its nest. We saw the eggs that were laid. We wondered later of the care it gave its young. Often we told stories of the Father. I told them to the child and the child told them again to me. We told them, the child and I, over and over again. Sometimes we stopped to rest, leaning against the Father's trees, letting his cool air touch our brows, and never speaking. And then, in the twilight, we met the Father. The child's eyes shone. He looked lovingly, trustingly, and eagerly up into the Father's face. He put his hand into the Father's hand. I was for the moment forgotten. I was content.*

It is the spirit of the third paragraph that is the essence of the Christian initiation process, the catechumenal model as we have come to know it. It provides the time needed for the person to offer their best to the one seeking, learning, being formed in the faith. If more of us can become aware of this freedom of unlimited time, learn to take it on and wear it, the more naturally evangelization and conversion of others and ourselves will follow. I have often wondered how Jesus evangelized. I see him inviting not mandating, explaining not expecting or assuming, encouraging not confusing or intimidating, compassionate not condemning, challenging but not making things impossible. What do you hear and see him doing in the Scriptures?

Working with the children and youth we had many activities and games we would use during the sessions to compliment the message. Some of these games and activities were workable with the adults as well. There are many resources available for use. It is important to be looking with a creative mind. I remember looking for a game for a birthday party once, and I came across a game that was considered low in body movement. As I read it I realized that it could be used in another venue for the children and youth in our sessions. All I needed to do was change the topic to what we were sharing about and come up with a few questions. The group is still using this today. We since have adapted the format of the original game to use with many topics and in different events with the children and youth. I attended a Faith Formation Conference one year and was introduced to ways of using improvisation. This workshop, given by Douglas Leal, was absolutely filled with ideas. I have used his material and inspiration throughout the years even with the adults in their sessions. Needless to say, the creativity available to us is limitless. We just need to watch and be adaptable to what the Spirit places in front of us.

Once a year we hold an overnight retreat for the adults and a day of retreat for the children and youth before the rite of sending of the catechumens to election. It is the custom for this rite to take place on the First Sunday of Lent. This means that you must plan in advance not only your retreat or day of reflection date with the participants, but all that comes in preparation for the rite. If someone is not ready for this rite two weeks before, they will not be receiving the sacraments during that Easter. It may be the next year. We are not in a hurry. Right?

How do we determine if the participants are ready to move forward to this rite? Once again, it is through the prayerful process of discernment that was introduced to the participants and to their sponsors earlier in the process. The team has already been discerning throughout the many sessions and times shared in discussion, prayer, and reflections by being present to the participants. There are definite ways of clarifying readiness; one is to hold another conversation with each person participating in the process. This needs to be done before the First Sunday of Lent.

Retreats or days of reflection are something that evolve in the process. We started out just like everyone else; a few people who gave their time and did their best because they cared. Depending on your situation with the number of team members, sponsors may be helpful on such an occasion. You may decide to invite them for all or for a portion of the retreat or day of reflection. Their knowledge of their candidate or catechumen can be very helpful to you if you are short on time or availability. Also asking the sponsors to write a letter of character witness regarding their candidate or catechumen can be helpful to you and to them. Giving a few guidance questions during the sponsor training in preparation for the rites of the Lenten season can aid them in this. The questions plus participation in the day of reflection or retreat with their candidate or catechumen, in addition to the time already spent, gives them the ability to witness to the changes and challenges they have seen in the life of the individuals. I have used this with sponsors for adults as well as for children and youth.

Thomas Morris' book, *RCIA, Transforming the Church*, has an entire chapter with direction on discernment for all involved in the process. We adapted his questions to the level

of understanding for the children, youth, and adults. The
answers to the questions give much insight regarding the
person's spiritual standing. The participants' responses to the
questions were very positive. It gave them a better picture
of their journey. These same questions can be reframed for
the sponsors as well. The sponsors can reflect on them in
order to give witness to the conversion of their participants.
Remember also that the rite book, paragraph 42 specifies the
prerequisites for moving forward to the second period. The rite
book #206 - #217 offers great reflection for the team regarding
preparation for the initiation rites. The team needs to reflect
on this material first before presenting it to those preparing
for the rites. As the team reflects and shares with one another,
they will naturally come to better appreciate the reflection
and sharing of the participants. This is also a catechesis, a
formation, for the team. When the team is well-formed in
their faith, in the process, and in an understanding of the
liturgical rites, it will affect how the participants are formed.

CHAPTER EIGHT:

HOW NECESSARY IS A TEAM?

The majority of parishes in my own diocese seem to have one staff person in charge of the overall process for adults. Very few also have charge of the process for children or youth. The popular thought seems to be to mainstream the children or youth within their own age groups and offer the needed preparation for the rites outside of their regular catechesis. Not many catechists are trained in the model of the Christian initiation process, so the usual catechetical method is used. The catechists are faced with a mixture of needs in their sessions and the process gives way to being a program. If the catechist is trained in the rites of Christian initiation process there can be a significant difference. The catechumenal model is spoken of often in the church, but unfortunately not experienced in much of the training for catechists. In past years, if a person on the team was interested, I encouraged them to attend one of the North American Forum Institutes held across the United States. The forum played a very important part in developing and implementing what we know today as the model for the catechumenate. The institute offered training and a deeper understanding into the fullness of the process and the rites to be celebrated. Since the forum has been discontinued, it is important that each diocese or parish offer some form of training and guidance for those serving in this ministry.

To answer the question if a team is necessary, bluntly— YES! No one person can offer the amount of time and energy necessary for the process to serve well the people who participate, unless you have a very limited number of participants and all one age group. When there are adults, youth, and children, you are also working with and serving those who come with them: spouses, families, parents, and siblings. The other facet of this process is that of the community family. How can one person feed all those who are coming to participate in the process as well as offer information and formation to the community? This is another reason having team members is important. One can begin by calling forward members in the community to serve. One of the best ways of finding team members is to invite those who answer the call to sponsor or the parents of children already initiated. When you hear how important the process has been to the sponsor or parent, as well as to the participant, that is an open invitation for you to return an invitation to them. If, in your observation of the sponsors and parents, you have seen some skills or gifts that would be useful in bringing others to the faith, use the opportunity to invite them to consider being part of the team. Giving them time to consider is important; however, if they hear your invitation as a positive reinforcement of the gifts you have seen in them, they will more likely feel called to take part on the team. Once you have your first two or three team members, then it is by word of mouth, personal referrals, and invitation from you and the team that others will become part of the ministry.

I took the advice of my mentor and called or personally invited individuals to an appointment with me in my office. I would state over the phone, or in person, that there was an important matter that I wished to take up with them. Would there be a day in the week that we could meet? As we met I would let them know how thankful I was to them for taking the time to meet and that I was appreciative of their efforts in whatever other ministry or event I had witnessed them taking part in. I would then let them know some of the importance of the catechumenate process to the community, and how the ministry affects the whole community. Then I would ask them to consider being part of the team for the process. I gave them information to read over that would offer a deeper understanding of the different periods of the process. We discussed the different age levels and the days and times that might or might not work with their schedules.

One of the important things about a team is that not all the functions are the same. Just as the gifts of individuals are different, so are the different areas of the process. The specific period sessions did have need of trained catechists, but not all are called to be catechists. Some are called to lead others in prayer, Scripture, retreats, or dismissals, and others have the gift of hospitality. Just as there were a few who took to recruiting and training sponsors, those on hospitality were the ones to notice when a catechumen or candidate was absent, needed a card of encouragement, or was celebrating a birthday, etc. The ministry of hospitality is the first and most important effort of evangelization because it is the first personal interaction between the participant and the team.

Once we had a number of team members, an enrichment session with them was offered three times a year. This would be for the continued training of the team members as well as for personal spiritual nourishment for their own journey in the process. In the beginning much of the focus of our time would be about discovering the personal gifts and skills each brought to the process. As this was recognized, they would then serve in the appropriate areas. Once this starts, there is no rest. The team is in need of constant nourishment. If you as director cannot offer this, I suggest finding someone in your parish or diocese who can. Bring them in to offer a day or evening of team feeding.

About five years into the evolution of the process we had teams for catechumenate adults, precatechumenate adults, catechumenate children and youth, precatechumenate children and youth, dismissal, and sponsors; six small individualized teams within one large team. There were at times around twenty-one people serving on the large team. We also had our drought years with eleven people. But even the lowest number was more than one. This looks good; however each time we seemed to have a team trained, something in life would happen and someone would move, be transferred, or some event would take place to force adjustments to be made.

I remember Fr. James Dunning saying that you should never ask another to do something you are not willing to do. This stuck in my brain for a long time. Working with the team helped me understand this. As team members we never asked any participant to reflect, pray, sing, read, or take part in anything that we would not. So, at our sessions you would find all team members fully participating in anything we asked the participants to do. There were many planning meetings when we would put together a reflection sheet and during the session hand it out to all present. One of the team members would look at the others and say, "We thought of this? This is hard!"

Team training and enrichment is necessary throughout this entire process. The feeding of the spirit is very important for those who are working in this area, because they are required to open themselves up and be vulnerable. For a team member to do this means offering up their experience of life and energy to the life of another. This does not mean uncovering their soul each time they share. However it does mean that each time they share or lead, they are willing to give over something of "self" to aid the others' sharing and growth in faith.

The longer the participant is in the process, the more of their life is shared, the closer they come to uncovering the truth of who they are. This brings the person to an acknowledgment of revealing Christ in their lives, which confirms a conversion of the heart. We have witnessed this in many adults, youth, and children.

Team members are those who guide, facilitate, walk, hold hands, listen, pray, and do all that is necessary to foster the conversion in another. However, this does not take place in a limited amount of time and space. It can only take place if a generous amount of time is given to the person journeying in the process, as well as for training for the team members.

Our main Scripture citation adopted early in the establishment of the team process and their formation was that of Psalms 1:1-3. It came to us as part of our own enlightenment in the process, and we began to use it for ourselves in meetings, formations, and retreats as well as for the parents, children, and adults in the process. The verses read as follows:

> Happy are those who do not follow
>> the counsel of the wicked,
>> Nor go the way of sinners,
>> nor sit in company with scoffers.
> Rather the law of the LORD is their joy;
>> *God's law they study day and night.*
> *They are like a tree*
>> *planted near streams of water,*
>> *that yields its fruit in season;*

Its leaves never wither;
whatever they do prospers (italics mine).

This translation comes from the New American Bible, and even though each Bible may have a different way of translating this verse, each states the same message. "That yields its fruit in season" was the key. This was a "sign" to us as a team that time was needed for each person, even ourselves. It was easy for us as team to begin to meditate on this for ourselves as we journeyed in our own spiritual growth, realizing that none of us, as trained as we might be, educated, wise, experienced, or religious, were finished learning or growing in our faith. Naturally the message came into use during our sessions with parents—those anxious for their child to receive the sacraments as soon as possible. We introduced it to our children and youth who were still asking the basic questions of who Jesus was really, and what did he have to do with their lives today. We used it with our adults, challenging some for the first time and others for the millionth time regarding their values in relationship to this world and their own morality.

The Psalms reading happens to be included in the Mass of St. Ignatius of Loyola. I found this out by accident while visiting Rome for the first time, attending the beatification of Mother Teresa. We were there because a priest friend of ours was able to take us to the room of St. Ignatius and there celebrate Mass with a few friends. I was taken by surprise that this was the Psalm written into St. Ignatius' Mass. However, thinking upon this, why not? Did he not suffer a "loud" conversion? Did he not know and experience the hand of God in process with him? Did he not know first hand the transformation of the heart and the time it takes?

Chapter Nine:

Interviews and Conversations in the Process

The word interview frequently is used with the idea of applying for a job. When someone calls the church, for information or formation in the faith, unlike applying for a job, it is the RCIA director or representative on the team and the visiting person interviewing each other. The director holds this conversation or interview with the individual to ascertain their motives, interest, and desire to enter into the process or program established in the church, and we listen to be able to understand their needs. They interview us to make a decision on whether they are ready to enter into such a program or process and if we represent the parish they would want to attend as members. The word conversation could be a better word to use; however, if left to the understanding of only having a conversation with another, the information the director seeks may not be obtained. Because many adults who come are busy, they will not want to spend an hour for such a conversation; they would like some expedience with their time.

It is helpful to have a short form asking for personal information including a few other items for your own knowledge. The importance of these moments is that of personal encounter. It may all start over the phone or even the Internet; however the personal encounter is as necessary as it was 2000 years ago. When anyone had an encounter with Jesus, it was memorable, whether they were transformed or not. We, who have answered a call to serve, serve Christ; it is he who encounters through us each person who desires faith. We are usually the first ones to welcome, listen, ask, challenge, invite, share, pray, and even cry with those searching.

The first encounter is for basic information; hopefully some of the individual's personal story will be revealed. Those sticky things like being married before or cohabitating with another may be mentioned. If they are in this irregular living situation, then the person holding the conversation can mention some of what will be necessary for the person in the future. However, it is usually a little too early for all this information at the first meeting. The person seeking needs to get started first, and after all, we are not in a hurry.

The following information is suggested:

NAME OF PARISH

RITE OF CHRISTIAN INITIATION OF ADULTS

Date: _____

Name: _____

Phone: _____ Cell: _____ Work: _____

Email: _____

Address: _____

_____

Birth Date: _____

Status: Married ___ Single ___ Divorced ___ Widowed ___

Baptized: Yes ___ No ___

Church of Baptism: _____

Address of Church: _____

_____

Date of Marriage: _____

Place of Marriage: _____

Name of Spouse: _____

How Many Children? _____

What is the reason you are here today?

_____

_____

What kind of religious or spiritual instruction have you had before?

_____

_____

    This information is adequate for the leader as the person begins the process. As a leader, you have the necessary contact information. If you need to call the home, you have the spouse's name, you have the status of marriage, and you know if there are children. You also know their baptismal status, what church the baptism was in, why they have come to see you (their motives or desires), and what kind of instruction or experience of any religion they have had in their past. This information, along with all that is shared in your dialogue with the person, will help you take the next step. Together they give you the information needed to know how much formation may be needed for the individual and into which period of the process the person may be ready to enter.

I remember a gentleman in his thirties who made an appointment with the director of faith formation to sign up his infant son for baptism. He arrived and they began to share in conversation, including filling out the basic contact form. When he finished giving the information needed, the director began to share about the baptismal sessions and what their content would cover. As he listened he said that his wife was not Catholic, and he would be the one bringing his son into the faith. The director had taken notice on the form that his last faith formation had been for first Holy Communion, when he was seven years old. She inquired about his attendance at Mass during the many years between then and the present. The man then stated that maybe he should look into his own faith before having his son baptized. Since he would be the one offering the faith support for his son, he should make sure he knew what he was talking about.

The interviews and conversations are not only important, but necessary. Along with the basic information form, we have ears to hear and hearts of compassion. These are our tools for this personal time with others. In the above story it was the person who came to recognize what was needed to build a strong faith, not only for his son, but also for his family. He did join the adult confirmation sessions and celebrated confirmation during the Easter Season. We did not make him wait, nor did we rush him through this process. He had some past faith formation, studies during college, and the desire to continue nourishing his faith. When he looks back today he says, "I wouldn't do it any differently. I needed to do what I did."

If the person is new to the parish or the faith tradition, being part of the precatechumenate is important for at least a short time. This will give the individual time to know the community of the parish during liturgy and the group they are a part of in the process. This is part of their evangelization period, and can only broaden their journey. During this time you too have the time to ascertain whether there is more under the surface that was missed during the conversation you had with them. Are there more issues or concerns verbalized in the sessions from this person that cause you to think this person needs a longer time in the first period? Is their attendance and participation what you expected? Are they attending Mass? When we give the individuals time for growth in faith, we have time to know and serve their needs as their faith develops.

A young man named Kevin came in for a conversation with me about the process. It was the first of our conversations and he came with his fiancée. During our time together he was the only one who spoke English and she spoke to him only in Vietnamese. I assumed that she did not speak English, which was not true. She was educated and could speak in three languages, but that meeting was for Kevin. During the conversation with Kevin he told a story of meeting her father. They had traveled for a Thanksgiving celebration to be with her family. It was the first time they were to meet him. On one occasion his fiancée's father asked Kevin to take a walk with him. As they walked, the father stated that his entire family had been Catholic all their lives, that her mother's family had been Catholic all their lives. He was expecting his daughter to marry in the Catholic Church. Kevin was not baptized, and the father wanted to know what his plans were. Kevin looked at me and said that it was at that moment he realized he "needed to learn to love the God that his fiancée loved if he were to marry her." What wonderful truth Kevin shared with me in that moment! It was three years later that Kevin came into the Catholic Church through full initiation. Today they are married and have a growing family. Had I only handed him a form to fill out without taking time to listen, there would have been little gained. Had I limited our conversation to only what I wanted to talk about, the full picture would not have been given for my own discernment as a leader.

Over the years we found that more than one personal conversation between the director or team member and participant was important and necessary. Many were scheduled into the session time, but others were informal when a participant needed to talk. The scheduled ones were the initial conversation, another before the period of entering the catechumenate, and one more before the period of purification and enlightenment. Each one had a different purpose and was unique to where the person had been in their journey recently, and where they were moving to. Before each conversation the participant, adult or child, was given a reflection sheet or booklet to take home or to use during a session to aid them in preparation for their decision, to offer them an opportunity for thought and prayer to discern if they should move forward in the process. Many of the questions we used were adapted from those found in the book called *The RCIA: Transforming the Church* by Thomas Morris. This book is a useful commentary for the *Rite of Christian Initiation of Adults*. Each period is examined along with the rites. Reading this alongside the rite book gave us as a team a positive and clear direction.

Time is important and there seems to be little of it when holding more than one position. If you are a director or coordinator in such a situation, don't lose hope. I keep hearing from those working in the church, "I don't have enough time," "I don't have enough energy for that, too," "I have been here seven days this week; don't I deserve one day of rest?" What can be done if this is your situation, so that you can offer the best possible process? We all need to remind ourselves that any process is better than none. So we do our best and are as creative as we can be. The one-day, one-person-at-a-time theory is good—hold on to it. I do know that I learned while "on the job," which is what most of us do. We in the church have at our fingertips numerous possible volunteers to help us. These people may not all be as trained as we'd like them to be, but their hearts are willing.

If your time with the individuals is too short, then one thing you can do is to rely on their sponsors, parents, spouses, or community companions for some feedback. This is why the training for the sponsors, parents, and all involved is so vital. They come to realize the importance of their role as sponsor or godparent in the process. The kind of feedback needed can be communicated in the letters of witness or in the reflection sheets that are part of the sessions. During the training sessions with the sponsors and others, time can be included for sharing concerns, needs, and issues they face with the person they are supporting.

As mentioned, we would hand out sheets for reflection during the sessions to generate discussion; otherwise, we would send the sheets home for "faith work," to be returned at the next session. In this way we were able to find out what they were thinking and feeling in a more individual manner. During the entire process, even during the precatechumenate, this is a helpful tool. We also found that the individuals would save their reflection work. We began offering pocket folders for this material so they could later read all they had written previously to see how their journey was going. Sometimes I have encountered people who were in my sessions, and they say they still have all the papers they worked on. This is a compliment to me and to them. It tells them how much they have grown since they began this journey of faith in a formal way, and where they are today. This can also become a tool for discernment in their continued faith growth. As each of us grows in our faith it is important at times to pause to see where we are in our journey. We need to take time to ask questions and to nourish our hungers and thirsts.

During the sessions one learns a lot from observing and listening. As director or coordinator, allow time for yourself to visit the sessions as your schedule allows. During your visit you can observe the catechists and the relationship they have built with the participants. As an observer you can also witness firsthand some of the actions, questions, and interactions of all present. If you are consistent in your visits, they will not be bothered by your presence. What you can gather from your own interaction with the participants, as well as from any written material, will help in your final assessment of their readiness, to consider along with the assessments of those who have traveled with them consistently.

One other reason for a conversation with participants, especially adults, is that of marital or cohabitation issues. I realize these topics are uncomfortable to talk about and sometimes cause embarrassment. However, as coordinators or directors, we are responsible to give the best direction of the church for the faith of the individual. If we do not stand up for the values of the church, then we may as well put aside all other teaching we do. The church views marriage as a sacrament, and we must value this from the very beginning of our interactions with individuals. When is the right time to find out that a participant may be living with someone outside of marriage? After a few years of experience, I began to read more on this subject so that I could be present to the individuals in their situation, and also gently challenge them. This is a pastoral encounter. It is an encounter where your primary purpose is to hold the individuals dear and precious, and yet firmly and truthfully offer them a call to change. This must come from your own heart, filled with love for those who want Christ in their lives. I have had a number of these experiences, but the first shall remain in my heart forever.

She was a participant in the adult process and he was her sponsor. They had been engaged for a year or so and lived together. The way I found out was that she had already filled out the information form when we first met. When he came to the first sponsor formation he filled out a form as well and the address matched. Consequently, I knew a call was needed. Since this was the first rite she was going through and we were well into the preparation, I decided to wait until after the rite. So, at the beginning of the catechumenate period I called and invited them both to my office. They were curious as to why we needed to meet, and I stated that it was a personal matter. We met informally in my office one evening after their work hours. I prepared some hot water for tea or coffee. We got comfortable and I began with the matter at hand, stating that I realized they lived together, having found this out by their same address. I didn't want them to stumble, so I kept on talking. I brought up the matter of the church teaching and how the church calls us to a higher standard. I shared that naturally the church was not going to follow them home; they were called to enter into prayer over this matter. Whether they made a change or not was up to them; however, it was my duty to make them aware of the teaching so they could decide. We discussed at some length what the *Catechism of the Catholic Church* stated and how we are all called to the ideal. Then we hugged and I sent them home to pray. They seemed to be fine during the many sessions following this conversation, but I never knew exactly what they had decided. She was initiated for almost four months before I heard from them. They were getting married and they wanted to meet. We met at my office again, and this time he was overwhelmingly excited. He couldn't wait to let me know how happy he was they were getting married because his back was killing him! He had been sleeping on the couch for a year! Also, her mother had made an extended visit and was still with them! We all laughed! They took the challenge as a personal call. They were the ones who made the decision. When given the opportunity to hear and spend time with truth, most people will value truth.

CHAPTER TEN:

DAYS OF REFLECTION AND RETREATS

It is so much fun to introduce people to a retreat, no matter what their age. Most of the participants have no idea what they are coming to, but they show up anyway. Then the day begins, and by the end they are ready to stay or begin another. With the children we offered day retreats, from 9:00am to 4:00pm on the church grounds. We could usually find a large space with a connected kitchen. This would serve as our food, activity, game, and discussion area. If it was available, we used the chapel or church during the day for prayer, reflection, Scripture, and sharing. The children always brought their lunches, but we offered breakfast-type foods in the morning and snacks in the afternoon, along with beverages. It would have been easy to script one or two retreats and just pull them out of the file as needed, but that was not what we felt was necessary. We wanted the retreat to speak to those attending each year, so some things had to be adjusted or changed. The retreat also had to fit with the time of year and what the church was celebrating.

The children experienced two retreats during the precatechumenate period and one during the catechumenate period. The first one in the precatechumenate was for community building, focusing on our connection with each other. The time of year determined the theme of the retreat. It could be offered close to the Feast of the Epiphany and speak to discipleship, or it could be during Lent and build upon our need for prayer. We determined what was best by our experience of each group.

One year we were blessed with two children who shared the experience of being deaf. They had each gone through different tests and surgeries for their handicap. It was the day of their first retreat during the month of November. It was a nice day, so we had games for the group during a break period outside in the field. At the end of our game time we were all going back into the hall for the next activity. These two happened to lag behind and were helping me carry back all the things we had used. Suddenly the young boy stopped and began to yell in an angry manner that he was never going to be right, that he had no friends, and that he couldn't do anything! She, being a little older, dropped what she was carrying and asked what he meant by all he was saying. He began by telling her about his deafness, the tubes in his ears and still not being able to talk like all the other kids. She placed her hand on his shoulder and said, "You think you're all alone? You are not. Feel my ears." He reached up and felt the tubes behind her ears. Looking directly into his eyes, she said, "You're no different from me. We are the same; I have the same tubes in my ears and talk like you do. I have just had a few more years of schooling." It was then that community began to take place for them. They had something in common and could share on a level that others would not always understand. I was blessed to be present and listening.

The second retreat for children during the precatechumenate period was part of their preparation for the rite of acceptance and/or the rite of welcome. The themes came from the focus of the rite in the *Rite of Christian Initiation of Adults* document. The gospel as a way of life and the cross are important to the rite, and these were the two themes of the retreat.

The retreat for the children in the catechumenate was before Lent, before the rite of sending to the rite of election. This retreat focused on the period of purification and enlightenment. We addressed all that the rite required for the participant so that they could answer with their "yes" to follow Christ. It was an introduction to their final preparation for the sacraments. During this retreat each participant wrote a short letter to our pastor stating their readiness for the sacraments and why they felt ready at this time. If there was anyone who did not feel ready to move forward at this time, they were invited to say so in their letter. Usually I or another team member would already have a good idea as to who would be moving forward and who would not. By their attendance, faith work, participation, and encounters in discussion we could have good insight into each child and where they were in their journey. However, I learned to remain open, as there is always room for surprise. Sometimes it is the child that teaches.

Christopher was a fifth grader who came to us, brought by his mother. He had been baptized in the Catholic tradition, his mother was Catholic, and his father Jewish. Christopher had many questions. When he first began in the precatechumenate he was full of questions about the faith. We answered the best we could, introduced him to his first Bible, and he started a prayer journal of his own. It contained his favorite prayers of the church mixed in with some of his own. We met at the end of the first year. He and his mother were excited to look at moving forward. I too felt that Christopher was ready for the challenge. The catechumenate period began and we watched him go through many changes. His interest was still present, but he was challenged to grow in a different way than the other children that year. His father died suddenly in the fall. The entire group gathered around Christopher and his mother, giving prayer and support in many ways. By March that year I was meeting with the children and using one-on-one conversations to gain insight as to their readiness. It was during my meeting with Christopher that he stated he was not ready to move forward. I listened and suggested that he talk this over with his mother and sponsor. Later in the week his mother called and we made an appointment to meet. At 3:30 in the afternoon on a school day Christopher, his mother, and sponsor all entered my office. We sat down and immediately Christopher stated aloud again that he was not ready to move forward. His mother and sponsor both stated in turn that they had been talking with Christopher about this and that he was quite certain. I asked Christopher if he knew exactly the reasons for his feelings at this time, and he replied "yes." I gave him the option of saying his reasons aloud or writing them in a letter to me. He chose to write a letter. As they left that day, I felt like I was witnessing something of a mystery, God's hand working in this child. The letter was delivered to the office the next afternoon. As I opened the letter I was anxious. I remember feeling that I was about to see something special. It was. Christopher wrote,

> *Dear Mrs. Blessie,*
> *You remember my dad dying? I know he is in heaven. Someday I want to see him again and mom said that I would. She also said that if I am not sure of Jesus in the bread that I needed to stay in the class. I think she is right. I love Jesus but I need more time to see him in the bread. Then I will be sure to see my dad again. This is the reason for me staying in your class and waiting till next year.*
> *Your friend, Christopher*

Christopher did, in fact, receive the sacraments the next Easter. He was right. He needed the time to form his connection to the community, to realize his importance in the Body of Christ.

Another experience was with a youth in seventh grade. He and his sister had been in the precatechumenate and then moved forward to the second period, the catechumenate. Neither of them had been baptized and they were preparing to receive the sacraments of initiation. Their mother was very involved with them in the process throughout the years. Because they did not have relatives who were Catholic, we found sponsors for them from within the community. All seemed to be going well. Then the day of the second retreat during the catechumenate period came. This retreat was before the period of purification and enlightenment. It was necessary for the children and youth to declare for themselves and us their readiness to continue forward to the Easter rites. We shared a full day together, all leading up to the time of the children and youth writing their letter of commitment. It was in this letter that each would state their readiness for going forward, or not, and why. The letter was written to the pastor or to me, since the two of us were the ones to read them. The children and youth were given the option of whom to address their letter so they could feel at ease. When the day ended I was anxious to take the letters and read them over carefully. That was when I discovered that this young man had stated that he was not ready. He did not feel in any way that he had learned enough or understood what all this was about for him. I was surprised since I felt certain of his readiness. The next day I called him and his mother to please come in and see me. During our visit, the mother was totally shocked. She was not aware of his feelings and tried to question him. Finally I asked if I could speak with him alone. She agreed and he seemed to be very happy that I invited this. In asking him what was going on, he stated that he had not been coming on his own accord. He was only coming for his mom. He had no intention of going through. Naturally I told him he would have to tell his mother and he said he would. Before leaving, I told him and his mother that I would let them discuss the matter for a few days, but that I would need to hear from them by the end of the week.

On that Friday morning, an envelope was pushed through the office mail slot with my name on it. It was a letter written by the youth stating his readiness for the sacraments. After speaking with the youth the first time, I had been certain that the mother would hear what he had to say and allow him to spend more time as needed in the process. However, it was the mother who convinced him that he was ready and that he needed to go forward. So I called the mother again. I asked for them both to meet with me again and they did. This time I had two letters in my hands; in front of his mother, I asked the youth which letter held his truth. After some silence he stated that the first was the truth, but that his mother really wanted him to do this and he didn't want her to be unhappy with him. As she listened, she began to realize he was only trying to make her happy. He did not receive the sacraments that year; his sister did. He continued for another two years before completing initiation.

All these experiences with these individuals taught me that it was not about our time, but God's time. Our job is to respect God's time with each participant, and to handle the different situations with gentleness but firmness.

During the precatechumenate with the adults, we try to have one day of reflection on a Saturday. This could include the regularly scheduled Saturday evening Mass with their sponsors or family and then a potluck dinner together. Even though they were in the precatchumenate, an important part of their formation was attending Mass. We found that sharing this experience together instilled a stronger commitment in them for understanding the faith. This kind of interaction helps to build trust and connection within the group.

On the nights both precatechumenate and catechumenate adult sessions occurred, we met together for snack time in order to encourage each group to mingle and get to know each other. We found this helped to create bonding and support for everyone. During the catechumenate period we offered an overnight retreat for the participants and some of the team. At first it was a day-long retreat, but we kept hearing from those participating how rewarding it was, and "if only there were more time," so we decided to change to the overnight retreat format. We found a location where we could keep down the cost if we did our own cooking. At first we wondered how this would work. We found out quickly that it was a great idea. We had sign-ups for the different meals so that everyone was taking part. Different team members supervised the kitchen helpers, and there was more bonding from cooking together than any game ever played! The retreat consisted of one or two witness talks about faith, reflection time, and experiential activities relating to the reflection and prayer. Because the retreat was held Saturday to Sunday, Mass was included at the retreat center earlier in the day, or the retreat would end with Mass in our parish.

If anyone ever wants an honest evaluation about something they have done, all they need do is ask those who participated. At the next session we handed out evaluation sheets for each participant to fill out. Because of their honesty we were able to offer a better retreat each year.

Chapter Eleven:

The Rite of Dismissal

This is a ministry in itself. It is not a time to leave Mass and go do what you want; it is a continuation of the celebration of the Mass, a time to work with the catechumens, those to be baptized, to break open God's living word among us. You will notice that this statement does not include the candidates, those who are already baptized in the Catholic tradition or another Christian tradition. By their baptism, each candidate is *required* to participate in the Prayers of the Faithful, the prayers of the community during the liturgy. Many of us are confused, and as a "courtesy" action or out of a concern that they will feel "left out," we include the candidates with the catechumens for the dismissal rite. The candidates, by virtue of their baptism, are called with the other already baptized members of the community to be present as the faithful. The faithful at this point in the liturgy have heard the word of God broken open for them, and now stand to pray together for all the church. Those who are not yet baptized are dismissed to further open the word of God for their lives.

We, the faithful, continue our struggle as one body to stand and pray together and ready ourselves to receive the Eucharist and to be sent forth. Our candidates are also standing with us in prayer as part of the one church. Many of them are also preparing themselves to receive the Eucharist. Their action is to pray with us and for us all, as we each go forward to receive, and dare to become all that God calls us to be. Because the church is apostolic, the candidates should learn to spread the gospel by witness of their own baptism.

They learn this from the community by being present during its liturgies and activities.

Most adult catechumenate catechesis sessions are held outside the dismissal time. There are some that continue with the catechesis session directly after the dismissal. Either is fine as long as they are distinct from each other, meaning that the catechumen knows when the dismissal ends and the formation session begins. Some parishes claim that the reason they dismiss the candidates during the dismissal rite is that they need as much formation in the word as do the catechumens. This may be true; however, dismissal is still for catechumens only. It is appropriate to spend fifteen minutes or more in a catechetical session breaking open the word and allowing some of the catechumens to share what they learned from their dismissal. What a way to begin their apostolic mission!

It is necessary to hold one or more formal training sessions for the leaders of this ministry of dismissal. Either the director or experienced team members will need to be present to guide the training. The focus of the training can be the following:

- What is dismissal?

- What is done during the dismissal rite?

- A shared experience of dismissal

- Distribution of any handouts helpful

There is a great vision for dismissal; one could call it an ideal. Imagine catechumens attending any liturgy with their family. During the liturgy, after the homily, the priest invites all catechumens present to come forward and he dismisses them to go and break open the word of God. There is also an awareness within this ideal community that someone is present and ready to walk out with the catechumens and lead the dismissal. This means that all catechumens would not have to be programmed into attending one specific Mass for the dismissal. All liturgies would be ready for this to take place. This vision provides and assumes ownership of the process by the entire community. All members would be ready to assist in the process. This vision can be the reality of what takes place. It will take more time, education, and an open attitude on the part of the current teams within the process, the priests, and the parish community.

A young woman entered our adult process, and after she went through the first rite, began attending the dismissals with the other catechumens. During this time her husband happened to go to Rome on business, and she accompanied him. They were in St. Peter's for Mass on Sunday, and as it happened all catechumens were called forward. She decided to go and just see what they do. She was the only English speaking catechumen, but there was a leader who translated for her. When Mass was finished she met up with her husband, and the priest who led the dismissal asked if they would like a personal tour of the basilica. Can you imagine such an experience? When she was sharing this experience with us during the next adult session, she was asked if she felt funny going forward for dismissal. She said no, and that she was happy she did. She would have missed out on quite a lot.

Dismissal is a time of a special form of catechesis; it is a time for faith sharing within the context of the readings of the liturgical celebration. It is always important to allow enough time for the catechumens to express what they have heard and understood from the gospel teaching. What they hear can make a difference in their conversion journey.

In my experience, some leaders do not have a full understanding that dismissal is a continuation of liturgy for the catechumens. They treat this time in a very relaxed manner, without proper reverence. There are other experiences where the leaders felt they had to catechecize as much as possible about the topic introduced in the reading. Neither is correct. Dismissal is first about the word of God. It is about the catechumens hearing the living word and asking what struggle or challenge it offers to their lives; what feelings or emotions are brought to the surface when they hear the reading; how the reading calls them to take action in their own lives. There are so many ideas and ways of opening up Scripture now, as well as ways of asking individuals to respond. I offer a few ideas here for you to use if you wish; however, knowing your group first is important. One kind of activity or medium never serves all, all the time.

Eight ideas for breaking open the Word with others:

1. Before reading the Scripture or story in the Bible, invite those in the group to picture themselves in the story or scene. Remind them that the word "gospel" means good news, and this reading has a message for them today, at this time in history. Read the story and ask how the story spoke to their lives today? What part of the story did they see themselves in or identify with?

2. If you are sharing with young children, before reading choose one phrase or word that brings focus to the message of what is read, and write it on the board or on a large piece of paper for all to see. Invite all the children to listen well to the story, remembering one word or sentence that sticks in their mind. When

done reading, invite each person, one at a time, to tell you or to write their word or sentence around your focus word or phrase. When everyone who wants to has participated, there is usually a great message that all can learn from. Take time to bring connection between the focus word or phrase you wrote and what the children have written.

3. Before reading the Scripture or story, you can hand out small pieces of paper to each person. As the reading is shared, they can write down the word or phrase that chooses them. Give time after reading for them to write down what they need to. Now read the story again. This time ask them to listen and write down one word, which challenges them to change in some way. Break up into small groups and share.

4. As an individual response, allow each person to have colors or markers and large drawing paper. Invite everyone to listen to the story and, while listening, to begin to draw their feelings, or how the message or story is affecting them. This may be by the use of color or image. All share when done.

5. Many of the gospels can be used in role-playing. I suggest you read the gospel, allowing the children to hear it first. Then invite the children to act out the parts, keeping in mind that their own personalities will come forward if they are not too shy. This is a wonderful way of showing the children the humanness of Jesus, in that he may have also shared some of the same feelings expressed. Allow for discussion, in large or small groups. (I have done this with adults as well.)

6. Rewriting the story or gospel in colloquial language is

a form of journal writing. This calls for an awareness of the message by the individual or group. It is necessary to read the word first, then allow enough time for the people to express themselves and put a message in writing. These are then used in further discussion. This is an excellent tool for sharing the many different ways God is heard and present to us in our lives.

7. This can be done as individuals or in small groups. Hand out paper to the group, one per person, or to each group. Ask them to draw a line down the center of the paper and write GIVES COMFORT at the top of the left column, and CALLS TO CHANGE at the top of the right column. Now read the gospel and invite them to write the words they hear that give comfort in the left column and those words that call them to change in the right column. Give time for sharing either in small groups or as a full group.

8. Read one verse of the Scripture at a time. Invite each person to write down a response on paper; it could be his or her feelings, a catchword, or a message they received. Pair up the individuals and invite one to be the reader and one the responder. Each reader reads only one verse at a time. The responder then reads their word, feelings or thought. When done they switch roles and repeat the same verse. When all pairs have completed sharing all verses, form a large group and ask for comments and how the word was heard. What challenge or discovery was received?

Most dismissals only last about fifteen to twenty minutes, so there is not enough time to do a lot. However, if the time is used well, all present can leave with a message in their hearts and minds that they are called to live. It is a time of evangelization with the good news.

Chapter Twelve:

Godparents and Sponsors

Another important ministry of the RCIA process is that of sponsor and godparent. Fundamentally, this is a call to the entire community to give support and prayer to those in this process. In the *Rite of Christian Initiation of Adults*, "Appendix III: National Statutes for the Catechumenate" (found in the back portion of the document), under the heading of Documentation, from the "Decree on the Church's Missionary Activity *Ad gentes* no. 14" we read:

> Christian initiation during the catechumenate is not the concern of catechists or priests alone, but of the whole community of believers and especially of godparents, so that from the outset the catechumens will have a sense of being part of the people of God. Moreover, because the Church's life is apostolic, catechumens should learn to take an active share in the evangelization and the building up of the Church through the witness of their life and the profession of their faith.

When the children, youth, or adults have been in the precatechumenate for some time and are beginning to consider moving forward into the second period, that is the time to bring in sponsors, if they are not already present. Parishes have many different ways of doing this. Some families have relatives who have already stepped up to sponsor the person. Maybe that relative has taken it very seriously and has been attending the precatechumenate already. If only we could have more people like that! However, that is not the usual situation. We are usually the ones searching and finding individuals, couples, or families to sponsor participants on the journey. This is a lot of work and, once again, enough work to establish a specific team of people to help. I chose three people, each of whom had gone through the process or sponsored before coming on the team. These three came to work together in the training of sponsors, godparents, and the parents of children or youth. They were also the ones looking for individuals in the community to serve as godparents or sponsors.

It is easy to confuse the roles of the godparent and sponsor. The godparent is the person who stands for the elect at baptism; the sponsor stands as a witness during the sacrament of confirmation. For the elect, the same person can serve as godparent and as sponsor. The two roles in the rites of Christian initiation for the elect are similar. They are to continue to encourage and be an example for the newly baptized in the practice of their faith.

I think the Christian initiation process challenges the godparent role for an infant. In the past, a relative would be asked or chosen to be the godparent and feel honored to have the role. However, many candidates shared experiences where there was never a connection with their godparent, no communication that led to a lasting, or any relationship. Consequently, the reason for being a godparent, to be present in the faith life of the individual, was absent. This also can be a challenge for anyone who serves as a sponsor or godparent to those participants who are catechumens.

In the catechumenate process, only those adults and children of "catechetical age" are fully initiated when ready. (*Rite of Christian Initiation of Adults*, #252) This means some formation is necessary for the person accepting the role of godparent and/or sponsor. Most people are still not accustomed to celebrating all three sacraments of initiation at the same time. They may be unfamiliar with children receiving baptism later than infancy. Some also have questions about someone younger than high school age celebrating the sacrament of confirmation.

When adults, youth, or children who have already been baptized as infants in the Catholic tradition enter into this process, they are given a catechesis that is founded upon the sacrament of their baptism. We give these individuals the name of candidates. The candidates can approach the godparent from their baptism and ask them to stand with them as a sponsor for confirmation. However I was always careful to ask the candidate about the involvement of the godparent in their life, and whether they were actually the one making that choice. My reason for this was that many parents would give a relative permission to be the godparent at the infant's baptism without any regard to their spiritual life, maybe because the relative asked and was liked. Consequently, as the child became older, the involvement may or may not have contributed to building the faith. Often an adult candidate wanted their spouse to sponsor them in the process. I never believed this should be encouraged due to the already existing roles of husband or wife in the relationship. I always ask them to take time and consider all options. They may have a great marriage but need to remember that their spouse already has had an important supportive role in their faith journey. They need to take this to prayer and not decide hastily. The few that did choose to have their spouses as their sponsors in my experience made positive decisions.

One year a young girl, around the age of thirteen, came

to enter the process. I met with her and her parents, and discovered that neither parent was Catholic. Her father was a humanist and her mother practiced a protestant tradition. It seemed that her grandmother was Catholic and had in some way influenced this young girl to become interested in looking into the Catholic Church. Her parents were very supportive, but it was her grandmother who watched over the faith building. This made a great impression upon the team and me because it showed the importance of having a person of strong faith to be the godparent or sponsor. Because the young girl was not baptized, it was necessary that the parents understand what she was asking, and that they attend all the sessions they could to give full permission. This was a lesson to all of us on the need for godparents or sponsors who practice their faith. What kind of example would this girl have if her grandmother were not strong in the faith? When we accept people from within or outside the community to godparent or sponsor others in the process, we must ask ourselves if the participants are getting the best possible.

During our years we found that very few participants had a relative able to sponsor them, nor did they know many people in the community well enough to ask. Often the participants would let us know they needed help finding a sponsor. This can be an awkward situation, bringing two strangers together for the first time to walk together in a journey of faith. Being a good sponsor requires being supported so as to support another. Naturally, some have a friend or family member who may be available; however, there are always those who do not, so each catechumenate team needs to decide how they will bring the two together. Will it be in a formal meeting with appetizers during a regular session? Will it be outside the session time at coffee and donuts where they are introduced and can talk together for the first time? Who arranges the meeting? Who answers all the questions? Does someone from the team meet with those who agree to sponsor a stranger before they meet the person? Does the team pair up the people with a sponsor, or do we just let them all meet and pair off as they happen to?

We decided to place a notice in our parish bulletin to invite community members to consider being sponsors. Those who responded were asked to attend a short meeting. At this event, we first thanked those attending and then outlined some of the requirements of sponsorship. We gave them a handout to take home and read. We asked them to pray about it for a week, and told them we would be in touch with them by phone to hear their final answer. Those who answered yes to the mission were asked whether they had decided to sponsor an adult, child, or youth in the process. Many were very definite as to what age group they would feel comfortable journeying with. For the adults, we would then invite the prospective sponsors to the sessions of the precatechumenate to meet people. They would be introduced as community companions, those willing to sponsor. Since this was early, at least two months before the first rite, there was time for sharing and conversing with each other. During break time we would see participants and sponsors pairing up in a natural way. One week before the rite, I would ask for names of sponsors and usually the adults were all covered. The team gathered in prayer to assign sponsors for the children and youth. Then the sponsors were invited to the next family gathering so that they could be introduced to the catechumen or candidate and his or her parents. It became a family experience for all involved.

We asked the sponsors to attend as often as they were able. If they could be there each week it was better for the participants. If they could commit to only once a month, then they were asked to make it consistent. We also mentioned that we expected they would be in contact with their participant outside the sessions, especially if they were unable to be present weekly. This contact could be by phone, card, or in church. The first and foremost goal we set for our sponsors was to establish a faith relationship with the participants. They were not expected to be at their birthdays or to go bowling with them. It was great if sponsors did happen to participate in these events, but the focus was on being present in their lives, especially their lives as part of the church community. Attending Mass and going to coffee and donuts to continue reflection together, or out to breakfast with the family was fine. We asked them to remember the focus on faith. It seemed to be helpful to the sponsors to know what and how much was expected of them. One of our more recent requirements was that each sponsor give us a copy of their own baptismal certificate. Their certificate was to be accompanied by a form they would fill out with their contact information as well as the name of the church where they received their first Holy Communion and sacrament of confirmation and the dates of these sacraments. This was a formal way of discovering which sponsors, if any, had not been baptized or fully initiated in the Catholic faith. It also helped us start earlier to help them in their understanding of the process. So many people are still ignorant of the rite of Christian initiation process. Once the sponsors understood their role and were on board, the better they were as sponsors.

During all our years, we have had only one person ask to change the sponsor whom we had assigned. We did comply due to necessity, however one is not bad. We also had one youth "fire" his uncle as a sponsor. We gave the youth a community sponsor who did the job very well. It is God who runs the ship. We just try our best to do our part.

The sponsor team calls companions from within the community to be present to the individuals seeking to become part of the church. The team holds four formation sessions for these sponsors/godparents during the year, one before each rite. The sponsors are required to attend each session. If they do not attend, I call them and we meet for a private session to provide the formation they need. At first this was frustrating, but it became a way to motivate them to attend the other scheduled formation sessions. The private session was intended to help them understand the importance of the role they had committed themselves to. When the first formation session was held, the team would present some background on the catechumenate for those considering sponsoring so that they understood the importance of their presence to their candidate or catechumen. The sponsors always requested more time to spend with their catechumens or candidates within the context of church. We did provide more time by having a Lenten retreat day for sponsors, catechumens, and candidates. However, the ideal is not always possible. What is important is the whole of the process and how it affects the conversion of all involved.

The formation sessions for the sponsors were for more than just knowing what the rite coming up was about and where they were to stand or what to say. Many people who were going to be sponsors had been Catholic most of their lives. They had been baptized as infants, gone through the sacramental preparation in their church, and received their first Holy Communion at the appropriate age. The majority of them had been confirmed during their high school years, a few during their adult years. What we had for the most part were people who had done what was expected and then gone on with their lives. They were husbands, wives, individuals with careers and very busy lives. They had tried their best to attend church on a regular basis and considered themselves good Catholics. Still, we consistently were told how much they appreciated the formation before each rite because it helped them understand their own faith better. As we heard this we understood that what we were offering was of importance not only to the participant in the process, but literally also to the faith of the sponsor. The more we were able to feed the faith of the sponsors, the better they would be able to be present for their candidate or catechumen.

Preparation for the rite of acceptance into the order of catechumens and/or the rite of welcome for the candidates offered a wealth of information and formation. Remembering that each rite holds within it a depth of meaning for the actions that take place, each rite needed to be presented to the sponsors for their own understanding and growth. We held the formation sessions for two hours approximately one week before the rite. The formation for the rite that the participants experienced needed to also be available to the sponsors.

We celebrated in combination the rite of acceptance for the catechumens and the rite of welcoming for those already baptized but uncatechized for many of my years of service. The important thing is preparing the community of the faithful to understand the different rites, and the difference between the candidates and the catechumens. This takes catechesis. A week or two before the rite, an explanatory announcement can be put into the bulletin, or made during the liturgies. An announcement during the liturgies reaches the majority of the community.

If you and your team are innovative, prior to the rite an open house for the community can be held with the candidates, catechumens, sponsors, and godparents to share some of the preparation in a form of reflection for all. Invitations to the community for this event can begin even a month before the rite. There are all kinds of ways a community can be catechized before the rites are celebrated.

When preparing the catechumens and candidates for the scrutinies during the Lenten season, we provide a similar experience for the sponsors during their sponsor formation. It is a formation for all who are sponsoring candidates and catechumens. It is important to offer deeper catechesis on the scrutiny to help the sponsors and larger community have a deeper awareness of what the participants are celebrating. At one of the sessions we invite everyone to participate in a closing ritual, which is an example of a scrutiny experience. The following is one such experience. We chose the gospel of the raising of Lazarus.

We were seated in a quiet space, dimly lit with only a candle and with incense in the air. The prayer table was wrapped in beige gauze material; a large wooden cross with nails in it was laid across the table. Each of us was called forward by our first name. Each person went forward and was given a long piece of sheeting measuring two feet long by four inches wide, symbolizing bandages. Our first name was written on the bandage. We were given a marker along with the bandage and sent back to our seat. When we all had received our bandage, the gospel was proclaimed. We sat in silence for a short time. We were invited to write on our bandages any barriers, sins, blockages we felt to reaching Christ. When we were done, we were then asked to tie the bandage on our wrist, ankle, arm, or leg so that we were a little uncomfortable with it; but not to tie it too tight. Then some of the team members began a reflective reading, one that was written from the perspective of Lazarus returning from the dead. This reflection led us to recognize how much Jesus loved Lazarus and how much he loves us now. A blessing followed, upon all our struggles, barriers, sins, and ways that we keep ourselves from stepping into the embrace of Christ. We were invited to take our bandages with us, to keep them as a reminder of our call to resurrection.

Whenever we offered such a ritual it was to bring the sponsor closer to the gospel, so they could then relate to the experience of their catechumen or candidate. Usually there was considerable discussion during the next session between the sponsors present and the participants, whether they were candidates or catechumens. The scrutinies touch us all. It is imperative to help the sponsors as well as the community come to see themselves as part of the experience as much as possible. If there is a way to offer a presentation on the scrutinies in your community through some program, or as a special workshop, it is recommended. The community of the faithful of the church are the witnesses of the Holy Spirit at work in the individuals who come forward as catechumens during the scrutinies. Think about it. These catechumens come before us, standing and then kneeling before the altar of Christ. They are in front of an entire assembly of their companions, and they place their entire selves into the hands of the Holy Spirit at that very moment. No matter what their thoughts, it is the faith and prayers of the community that overtake and immerse the lives of the catechumens into the movement of the Holy Spirit within them. The power of prayer does act, and change does take place for all present.

CHAPTER THIRTEEN:

THE RITES

When our parish first introduced the catechumenate process in 1981, we had only adults in the process. It wasn't until 1987 that we had a group of children and youth ready to celebrate the rites of initiation. At first, because they were not thought of as part of the overall catechumenate process, the children received their sacraments on the second Sunday of Easter. So, for a number of years the adults celebrated during the Easter Vigil and the children and youth the week after. We noticed that most of the music groups would happen to take off the week after Easter Sunday. We needed to find someone to provide music for us. We also noticed that within the community the excitement level of the celebration of the sacraments for the children and youth was different than that for the adults. This was disturbing to me. When the position of Director of the Catechumenate was offered to me, I was able to bring changes to the process, but not overnight.

The catechumenate model is one process that includes children, youth, and adults. The celebration of the rites needed to change. Even though each group met at a different time for catechesis, the rites could be celebrated for all catechumens and candidates within the process. So, for the first time we began to see children, youth, and adult catechumens take part in the rite of acceptance and the dismissals. We also witnessed children, youth, and adult candidates take part in the rite of welcome. This was a new experience for the community. A new awareness and understanding arose, and people asked questions.

One Sunday after the rite of acceptance, I was cleaning up and a young woman came up to me to share how it had touched her to see the blessing of the senses done for the children as well as for the adults. She was quite moved and decided to begin blessing her own children each day. This was the beginning for our community to witness all of the rites with children, youth, and adults.

As mentioned earlier, it is always a priority to keep the differences between catechumens and candidates clear for the community when celebrating a combined rite. I want to add that when celebrating a combined rite, it is necessary to keep all the information clear for those participating as well. This is especially important when working with children, youth, and adults in the process. Sometimes we can go overboard with our need to help a specific age level understand. When we take a rite and simplify the wording to make it more acceptable to the age of the children, for example, we need to be certain we are not watering down the meaning of the rite. Watering down weakens the meaning for all. If our preparation is done well, and we catechize to the rite itself, then very little change is needed.

This is particularly true of the scrutinies. Children and youth today are very aware of temptation and sin. It is our responsibility to help them be aware of sin in their lives, to take responsibility for it, change their actions, come to a conversion, and sin no more. We offer understanding and ownership through games, activities, handouts, retreats, songs, prayer, Scripture, and many other means. By the time the children and adults are ready to proceed to the rite of sending for the rite of election, they should be very familiar with the process and unafraid to dig deeper within themselves.

For the team, catechizing towards each rite means opening the book and reading it, so we understand it well enough that we can bring it to those who are preparing for it. As we open to the rite of acceptance in the RCIA document, we see an outline of the rite. It offers us an overview of actions that will take place for the participants. When we read about the participants' first acceptance of the gospel in the outline of the rite, we should ask ourselves what this requires us to do to prepare the participants. If we read that part in the rite, we will find different options that the priest can choose from for the rite. For the catechesis we are able to use these, or the one the priest will use, ahead of time. Then, during the rite, when the participants hear the words, they will strike a memory. They will not be just words. They will have heard them before and be able to take ownership of them. Further in the overview of the rite we see the "Signing of the Candidates with the Cross." Once again we can turn to this section in the rite and read over the different senses that are signed, taking into our own hearts the meaning of the words for each of the senses. Then again we can bring aspects of this into our preparation with the participants. This action also becomes something that is more than just words. It can become a living part of each of us, as we realize we are living signs of the cross of Christ.

There was one man who took quite a length of time in the process, about six years. We were all happy for him the day he was initiated. He had struggled and been challenged; but finally "light shone in his darkness." One day after he was initiated he came into the office and shared how much his journey had meant to him. He wanted to give something back to the process. I welcomed him to offer whatever he could, and to let me know when he decided what that would be. Months later, during the fall, he brought into the office a very large wooden cross. It was made out of his relatives' old fence. It was about 36" tall and 24" wide. It was nailed together, and an old worn out rope was tied over the place where the two pieces of wood met. It was an unattractive cross and, in fact, it came to be called the "ugly cross."

This cross became the favorite of a majority of participants through the years. It spoke just by being present in the room. We would use it for our prayers, especially in preparing for the rite of acceptance, and then again during Lent. On both occasions we saw reactions and responses from participants that only a visual can bring. Over the years, I would use the cross in retreat experiences with the children. They would write a prayerful response to a question on a small piece of paper and attach it to the cross with a nail. Some of the nails were hammered in so securely that they stuck and wouldn't come out, so they were left. We began using the cross with the nails for prayer rituals. One example was hanging a key from each nail; we invited people forward to take a key, and to leave something else on the nail in its place. During the three sessions of preparation for the rite of acceptance, we would end each session differently by using the cross.

The first time we invited each person in the circle to silently reach out and touch the cross in prayer. Then we closed with a blessing. The second time we again invited everyone into a circle, the sponsors standing with their participants, and invited each catechumen or candidate to let their sponsor hold the cross with them. Again this would take place in silent prayer. The third time we invited each person alone in the circle to hold the weight of the cross. This series was a progression that helped develop the meaning and acceptance of the cross in their lives.

There are times in this process when children, youth, and adults can come together. Celebrating the rites together is one area where it can happen in a natural way. We come to church and celebrate liturgy together as one family, all different ages and walks of life. This is the vision for the process as well. Days of reflection together, along with sponsors, are a great way of bringing the participants together. There are also many times when the adults and children shared dismissals together.

Holy Saturday is an important day for all in the process. We invited together those being received into the Catholic Church, those already baptized in the Catholic tradition, those who were our catechumens, and the adults who joined us to celebrate their confirmation. We began around 10:00 am and ended around 1:00 pm. The time together was meant to be a day of prayer for them, to help them to focus on the meaning of the day without outside disturbances. We did not invite parents or sponsors for this time. We also kept the day for fasting, offering only crackers, a little fruit, and juice. They knew that this was different from other days together by the lack of food! Our day would begin with prayer; then the gospel for the day would be proclaimed, followed by a time for sharing from hearing the reading.

During this event the catechumens were given time to reflect upon the baptismal vows they would proclaim "yes" to. The candidates to be received reflected on the profession of their faith. All were given time to reflect upon the Nicene Creed before reading it aloud as one voice. It was a statement in itself, given freely by all those joining in the walk, the passion walk. At this time, we would separate the children and youth from the adults. There would be special spaces to go to for further sharing at the level needed. The adults would continue to share with one another, looking back on their journey, the first call, and the encounter with Christ. As they looked back, they would examine what changes they saw. The children and youth would do something similar, but their experience would center on the Triduum. They were asked to think about their precatechumenate period, how they came to know others in the group and in the community, and how coming to know others affected their faith. They made a cross bookmark, wrote on it the names of community members who had made an impression upon them, and placed it in their Bibles. We asked them to follow us outside (on fair days). We had filled a child's pool with water and placed beach towels surrounding it for them to sit on. They removed their shoes and listened to the gospel reading from John where Jesus washes the disciples' feet. Then one by one they were called by name. A team member washed their feet in the water and then dried them with the towels. When done, a paper with one question was handed out to them. It asked, "How did you feel about having your feet washed today?" They were given time to write a response and then we shared in the large group.

We all returned to the hall, had a short break, and then came back together. The final time was spent with a reflection on the nails that pierced Christ's hands and feet. We were in silence; the reading was proclaimed while a nail was passed from one person to the next. Each would take time to inspect this nail. It measured 8" long and was considered to be a replica of the Roman nail that was used. Each year that we did this we noticed the profound seriousness of the children and youth. They did not take this lightly. Maybe it was having their feet washed first. I have no idea. But this reflection with the nail placed them into a particular space that showed on their faces, they knew the awesomeness of what Jesus had done for them. By this time the adults would return, we would close in a prayer, and send them all off for the day. Later that night we would celebrate at Vigil.

We celebrated the sacraments of initiation with the catechumens during the Easter Vigil. The candidates would be in the community of the faithful. The next week our candidates were received into the Roman Catholic Church, and those receiving their Confirmation and first Eucharist celebrated those sacraments as well. Both celebrations were with adults, youth, and children. A reception was held after each liturgy, and the community was a major part of the celebration. I discovered that there are some of us who are "vigil fans," meaning we cannot miss the vigil. There is just something about that night that is habit-forming. It can get inside your blood and hold you mesmerized for years. To be in the midst of something so ancient and yet so new at the same time is part of the mystery. I have always been happy that we celebrate this night with all ages, as throughout the years.

Always it is the attitude of the catechist, director, and the other leaders of the parish who make the vision possible or not. If we see nothing wrong with adults and children sharing in prayer and Scripture together, then they won't either. Our job is to educate ourselves to be ready for this to take place. We can run the agenda only for so long and then the Holy Spirit steps in and we are no longer in control. Our challenge is to see as Christ sees.

CHAPTER FOURTEEN:

SCRUTINIES

As you may realize by now, I am an advocate of celebrating all rites with children, youth, and adults together. All catechumens can celebrate these scrutiny rites together; it is the preparation that makes it possible. Preparation is not practicing with them what they say and do in the rite. Preparing them is getting down to the level where their hearts and minds are having challenging thoughts, questions, concerns, doubts, fears, and profound feelings about themselves, others, and God. Preparation is about guiding them into being confronted with where they are, with who their friends are, with how they act towards others, with the language they use, with how they see their body, with what they think, and with why they want to follow Jesus.

The *Rite of Christian Initiation of Adults*, #141 says:

> The scrutinies … are rites for self-searching and repentance and have above all a spiritual purpose. The scrutinies are meant to uncover, then heal all that is weak, defective, or sinful in the hearts of the elect; to bring out, then strengthen all that is upright, strong, and good.

This is about conversion taking place deep within the person. We, the catechists, directors, and facilitators, are in a unique and special position where we have the opportunity to walk with another in this period of the process. It does not matter their age, only their conversion of heart. We are those who have been invited to be a small part in their journey. We owe it to them to offer the absolute best we can to help them in preparation.

During the Children's Initiation Institute of the North American Forum I discovered a way to help in the preparation for the children and youth. I started it with them, and when I came to be the catechumenate director, we used it with the adults as well. During the period of purification and enlightenment in the process the catechesis is different from the other periods. This period is more like a retreat. It is a time for deeper reflection on the gospel readings and for prayer. We found ourselves looking more closely at the readings for the Lenten season and developing our sessions with them. We continued to break open the gospel from the previous Sunday in our session.

Our Lenten experience through the gospel readings begins with Jesus being tempted in the wilderness. Then we go with him to his transfiguration. There is the woman at the well, the man born blind, and the raising of Lazarus. Each of these is a conversion story for all of us. At the end of each session with children, youth, or adults, a ritual prayer would take place. We would pass out some form of paper with a question on it for all to answer. These answers were then brought forward or collected in a special manner to be read later in private. Some of these small papers went on the nails of the cross I mentioned earlier as a prayer response. These answers were to questions that would correspond to the next week's scrutiny. This meant we had to start collecting their responses during the session before the first scrutiny. It would be from these participants' responses that the litany for the scrutinies would be formed. Each week they would hear some of their own answers read aloud in the scrutiny intercessions, not knowing that it came from them. These were their personal answers, rewritten into a general format, and yet they connected the whole community.

At first some of the team felt this was too deep for the children. However, that thought was proven false. The children and youth never had any problem with answering the questions or expressing their feelings in a very truthful way. It was the adults who were more challenged with getting deeper. We as adults wear so much armor about us, and yet we want to walk without the weight. It is the children who were able to name it better than the adults. One year a child wrote that she was afraid of guns in her home. This was added to the litany without hesitation, and everyone prayed hard since so much has happened in our society regarding guns. We worded the phrase so that the child would hear her fear prayed over; however it was listed with other fears as well. We came to realize that children are sometimes more ready than adults to name their fears.

Chapter Fifteen:

Mystagogia, a Period of Breaking Open the Mystery

This word is a Greek word and the name of the last period of the process for neophytes, those just baptized. This period gives them a year to go within themselves and revisit the times, events, episodes, feelings, questions, etc. of their faith journey. This is an opportunity for them, their families, spouses, and sponsors to again return to those first meetings, see again the rites in their memories, celebrate where they have been, are, and will continue to journey.

Those of us who have been involved in this process for a while have experienced the high times of those receiving the sacraments, and then have experienced what seems to be a falling off in their attendance. Some say this is a graduation attitude. I choose to think that the spiritual high is not gone from the newly initiated; it is just society creeping in and taking over priorities. There is no cure; it is something that is inherent in our humanness, in the way we live. It may or may not be a fault. As catechists we have the opportunity to begin a process in the precatechumenate of replaying the spiritual events celebrated during their time of formation. It would be a model of the mystagogia experience, given early to introduce the importance of living out the mystery even later in their journey. Events to be remembered can be rituals used as part of a closing prayer, a parish day of prayer, or a special Mass celebrated for a feast day. Any one of these can be referred to or remembered during a session after sharing the event.

The North American Forum Institute, Beginnings and Beyond, did use the mystagogia experience each day after a rite was celebrated. Everyone present was invited to go back and remember with his or her senses what took place for them during the rite. We all shared in the remembering, with music, prayer, and words from the rite, some personal memories of something specific, the flowers, or incense, or any of what was present to us during our celebration. Then time was given for all to share what was brought up or experienced in our memories. It was through this exercise that we as a group could grow by the sharing and wearing of each other's experiences. It deepened the event and challenged the heart.

In remembering an experience, the senses are highlighted. Feelings are recalled; smells, words, sounds, tastes, and what was seen is remembered. As these come to the surface, memories are stimulated. The last period of the process is for reviewing the journey, seeing where they were, where they are, and how far they have come, and then for looking ahead, to see where they will be called to serve. It is this period that gives that person's search momentum. During the entire process I try to help the participants experience different events in our parish and sometimes outside the parish. If in planning the calendar you see that your parish is having a prayer service, Mass, concert, speaker, mission, etc., try to allow your participants to attend. This offers those events, not only for spiritual growth, but also for discussion about their growth within their own lives, and in connection with the community. There are many outside organizations that welcome the opportunity to give a tour and information to challenge areas of Christian teaching. I knew one group who visited a prison. It made such an impact on the group that they adopted the prison. They continue to be in contact with the inmates and authorities with visits and cards. Catholic

Charities and Sacred Heart Community Service are two places that we visited in San Jose, California. Both challenged the individuals on where they might be called to serve.

One year the team went with the adults in the process to Sacred Heart Community Service for a tour and some prayer. On a daily basis this organization helps fulfill the immediate needs of many people with food, clothing, etc. The night was wonderful. We had a delightful tour guide, who was very detailed and answered each question. After our tour we sat and discussed the challenges we face in serving our community. We said a prayer and began putting away chairs and saying good night. Everyone had left when the tour guide motioned to me to come see her before leaving. I went over and she told me that one gentleman in the group had come to her and said that at one time he had needed their services for food. He had taken out his card and placed it in her hand saying thank you; he did not need it anymore. He was in tears as he left. I was able to see where his card was hole punched for each time he took a meal. She and I hugged and gave another thank you to God. Another young woman on the same tour was so touched by the experience that she took it upon herself to begin a clothing drive at her place of work. She let others know to bring their used clothing on a certain day. She then packed up her truck, drove it over to Sacred Heart Community Service, and dropped off the clothing. She stated that she did this because she couldn't figure out how she could do anything else with her schedule.

Needless to say, mystagogia begins at different times for each person. We just need to allow them time for reflection and reconnecting. Many of us have for years tried to formalize this period and hold sessions after initiation. I did. I tried it on the same night, different nights, Sundays after Mass, once a month, twice a month, and finally decided that each person celebrates this period the way they are called to. I now believe that we are to meet with the neophytes through Pentecost, have a great sending forth, and then meet with those who continue to have a need. Those who are ready to fly should not be held back. If we hold them back, we need to be conscious of our reasons. If your parish has many events offered for the entire community, the newly initiated need to experience them. Maybe you can get together once in a while for discussion and sharing, or for a meal and reflection. But I do not believe we need to have formal sessions for a year. Once initiated, they are ready to experience the parish—all of it. We are their guides for rounding out their journey, finding where to use their talents and gifts. They need to be sent to see, hear, touch, smell, and feel.

We are taught in this journey that we all will go through darkness sometimes in our lives, but will reach the light when we walk in faith. It will be the others with us who give us strength when we are weak, prayers when we need them, and loving trust to continue our journey. Just as they will be there for us, we will be there for them. It is in being with the whole of church that the neophytes will find this to be true for them. Their faith will be strengthened by what they experience as will the church. All of us will connect with memories, recognizing together those moments we sat in the embrace of Christ, the loving Mystery.

Chapter Sixteen:

Conversion and/or Sacramental Formation

When I began working as a volunteer catechist, it was with the second graders. The curriculum for the year was their preparation for celebrating the sacraments of reconciliation and first Holy Communion. We began with the preparation for the sacrament of reconciliation early in the year, around October, and celebrated the sacrament in the month of November, just before Thanksgiving. Then, after the Advent and Christmas seasons, we began the preparation for first Eucharist, usually celebrated during the month of May. My first year was a year of learning about the sacraments that I had received only a year before and held dear. Teaching at the second grade level gave me a more concrete and clearer understanding. I found the formation of the children fun and exciting. Once in a while we would invite the parents to join their children for a session. They would come forward at the end of the session and say how much they appreciated my way of explaining, that even they could understand the meaning of the sacraments better. This said a lot to me. It said that people of adult age can take something intended for a child and allow it to bring them to a deeper level of understanding. This is what had taken place for me, and now I was hearing the same from other adults, who had been part of the Catholic Church since childhood. As the years continued, I increased my own knowledge, and continued to hear more appreciation expressed by other adults.

When my husband and I took on the process of initiation for the children and youth six years later, we brought the parents' comments to the attention of the director at the time. We wanted to make both the children and their parents part of the process, calling it a family process. I had noticed that the majority of parents of the second graders had allowed their own understanding of their faith to become stagnant. Their knowledge of the faith had not grown since they had last prepared for sacraments as a child. For most of them this was second grade, and for some high school.

So with the director's approval, we incorporated the parents into the process with the children in a unique way. We knew we wanted the children to have time with each other and to be able to build friendships, so we decided to have the parents as part of the process with the children every other week. We had the children for only nine months at first. In reality we had a program for the children and youth. We were to introduce them to the faith during the first three months and then prepare them for the sacraments of initiation. After going through this for two years, we asked our director to allow for more time. We did not feel that we were giving the children the best we could when limited to such a short period. We wanted to offer all the catechesis required by the process for the children and youth and not be so limited. We needed more time to form them in the faith. As we met, we shared what we had experienced with the parents. All agreed that the parents were the primary catechists of the children. Since parents are the primary catechists for their children, then we as church should equip them as such, offer them the appropriate time for any questions or issues of their own, and give them further material for building their own faith so they can share it with their children. It is the parents who drive and bring the children to church.

We were given permission to begin a two-year process for children and youth before the celebration of the rites of full initiation. Because the children and youth had only had their first year of catechesis, none were ready for initiation during the Easter Vigil that year. The next year many of the children and youth in the group expressed their readiness to move into the catechumenate period. They celebrated the rite of acceptance in November, the rite of sending on the First Sunday of Lent, and went to the cathedral to celebrate the rite of election. Then, during the Easter Vigil they were baptized, confirmed in the faith, and welcomed to their first Eucharist. We were all ecstatic and felt we had done a fantastic job with our first group. When these children and youth had entered the second year, we had another catechist helping us so we could take on another group for their first year. That way, each Easter from then on there were children and youth celebrating the sacraments of initiation along with the adults in the process.

We were three years into all of this when the reality of conversion became clearer. What if one child, third grade level, attends the first year and writes a letter at their retreat day stating they are not ready to move forward to the next period? What do you do when you have the child and parent in your office and you, with the parent, are trying to convince the child that it would be good to move forward, and they disagree? Does the child or youth have the right to make the decision? It states in *The RCIA: Transforming the Church* by Thomas Morris:

> The decision to celebrate the rite of acceptance
> ultimately rests in the hands of the individual inquirer.
> … The decision to choose to commit oneself to the

gospel within this Catholic community is made by the inquirer (p 70).

Naturally it is necessary that they discuss this with parents, sponsors, team members, and others involved in their journey. However, it is the inquirer who makes the final decision, even though they may be only in the third grade.

This issue called for a closer look at what we understood as conversion. If a child in the third grade can see they are not ready to move forward, for whatever reason, might not there be adults who feel the same? Is what we offer truly a process, one allowing the person's faith to evolve in God's time? Or, do we have a program that has expectations of everyone being ready to receive the sacraments at the same time? It is not we who convert others. We are the "tools" in service to the movement of the Holy Spirit within the heart of the individual whereby they experience a conversion of the heart. We are necessary to the extent that the Holy Spirit may use us. The divine Triune God could change the person's heart without us. However, humans need the human touch, directly or indirectly, in conversion events. In other words, we need each other. God has formed us that way. So, is it possible that within the individuals, the Holy Spirit may be moving and calling them to more understanding before taking another step? Are we, the director, team, parent, spouse, and sponsor, in communication with the individuals, able to understand and accept their need for more time? The process of conversion is different for each person, no matter his or her age.

It is easy to get caught up in the attitude that when the group has been attending for a length of time they are naturally ready to move on. This is the academic school model that we have adopted for many years. Conversion is a change of the heart, which then radically changes the way a person lives. If given the time to come into a relationship with God, Father/Jesus/Holy Spirit, whether child or adult, then the change within the heart may be longer lasting, stronger, and deeper. I have no studies to show for my opinion, only experience and observations through the years with individuals with whom I have come in contact.

Chapter Seventeen:

The Catechumenate Model and Those with Special Needs

I, and the team who served with me, were blessed through the years to have the attitude that we were able to learn and grow from each person's experience. It was not we who were doing all the teaching and those in our sessions doing all the learning. The catechumenal model is one where even those facilitating the sessions are expected to take full part with those new to the spiritual journey. So, as mentioned earlier, we did take part in the reflection sheets, the art projects, activities, field trips, and the sharing of life. If the team is open to learning from each person who enters the process, then an accepting attitude will characterize the entire group.

Special needs, physical handicaps, mental challenges, emotional disabilities, etc., are all a part of our lives because we live with others in this world. We all, in some way, have some special need. The challenge is to our thoughts and attitudes. For those of us with more apparent special needs, we fear being made fun of, not being accepted, standing out, being stared at, having too much fuss made over us, degrading comments, intimidating remarks, and much more. For those of us who encounter people with special needs, we become clumsy in our use of words, we wonder how to treat them, if they will understand us, how to deal with them. We feel sorry for them; we question their quality of life, and much more. Obviously the wall is thick and built with arrogance, ignorance, misdirected emotion, power, prejudice, etc. So, the question and challenge is, how to change the way we think of and see those with special needs? Do we see ourselves with special needs? How did Jesus respond to individuals with needs? When he heard the blind man calling out to him on the road, what happened? When his friends lowered the man who was crippled down from the roof, what did Jesus do? When the woman bleeding touched Jesus' robe, what did he say? When he heard that his friend Lazarus had died and was buried, how did Jesus respond?

We have been given the best example to follow: to invite, to accept as is, to offer the love and truth of Jesus and to let it grow. All of us on this journey grow together; no one grows alone. This example may be rather simple, however it is true.

We were in the process of remodeling our family room and were painting. Our daughter has a wonderful artistic eye and was helping with the color and design of the room. We had decided to have a textured wall over the fireplace, which she did, and then we painted it with an accent color. The color was a dark wine color, beautiful, but it stands out and is dark. The rest of the room is light rose beige, which is soft and calms the wine color. The stairway to the room has a wrought iron banister set in a large piece of wood. It seemed out of place. Our daughter said, "Paint it the dark wine color." We were surprised at first. She explained, "When you have something that stands out like an elephant in the middle of the room, then you bring it to the forefront to make it blend into the rest." I will say that to this day it really works. I can go down the stairs and not even notice the large piece of painted wood. My eye is drawn to the larger area of the room and to the accent wall. Instead of the banister wood piece standing out, it blends in with the beauty of the whole room.

I use this example because if the elephant is in the middle

of the room, it needs to be brought forward so that all can see, hear, touch, and feel it. It is like the young lady who complained about her wheelchair; everyone always noticed it and made such a fuss over her. Others could enter a room and not be noticed, but whenever she entered all eyes turned. I asked her what would happen if she painted the wheelchair red, had balloons and stickers all over it, would that be better? Then the eyes would really see something! She laughed and said that she would hate such a chair. She wouldn't be able to go anywhere without being noticed. So, then I asked her if having the chair might be part of her spiritual call, like having a mission that calls others forward? I know that the prophets of the Old Testament felt like God had given them something of a burden as well. They were not considered to be accomplished people of their day. But, God calls whomever God chooses to fulfill a purpose. God never calls us to be comfortable. We are people called to be filled with the Holy Spirit, the Breath of God, to move the hearts of others even while our own hearts are changing. Just as my banister blends into the colors of the room and serves its purpose, so does this young lady in her wheelchair blend in as she is accepted to serve her purpose in serving Christ.

Fr. John Aurelio, a priest who worked with children with special needs, once told a story about a young boy who would go traveling with his parents. He would always be in the back seat with his grandmother who traveled with them. As he would sit there, she would knit. He would hear the rhythm of the needles as they made their stitches. At times there would be a pause in the rhythm. Then she would pick up the rhythm again. He came to understand that during the times his grandmother would pause, she was trying to go back and pick up a stitch she had accidentally dropped. Later, when he would tell stories to children, one day a child asked him how God made them. He used this story to answer the child's question. However, at the part where his grandmother would go back to pick up the lost stitch, he would say that God would not, because God made all things perfect the first time. God would leave the missing stitch because God loved the original gift of life as it was.

I have a very special friend who will always be about the age of thirteen. She is now twenty-five and we still see each other and remember how we met. I was her teacher; she was eight years old at the time. She came into the sacramental preparation class so that she could receive her first communion. There were fifteen children in the class, and everyone knew that she was different. It wasn't because it was announced, but that she acted very loud sometimes and had the understanding of a younger child. During the year we were together I brought to the sessions many of the activities that I had learned from my Montessori training. I did not bring them only for this young girl, but for the whole class. It was a way to reach her as well as to offer all the children a special way to learn. Montessori teaching focuses on the senses of an individual to stimulate learning. This can be adapted for use in the catechumenal model as well. Children naturally want to eat, smell, touch, listen, and see all forms of things. Stimulating their senses in each session to give some understanding of the sacraments became a wonderful experience. We painted sidewalks with water in the afternoon sessions, we rubbed lotion into our arms and hands, we finger-painted with jello pudding, we made Scripture cupcakes, and we baked bread to share. Each activity was designed to cultivate the use of their senses and to bring their hearts and minds to know Jesus in the sacraments.

At the session during the first week of Lent the children were waiting to hear what we were going to do that day. I had brought with me to class a beautiful purple flower and had it in water on our prayer table. We had said our prayer and read the Bible story of Jesus going into the desert to be tempted. Our discussion of the story was lively. Then my young friend asked if she could smell the flower. I picked up the vase and offered a chance to smell it to her, and then to all the noses in the room as she proclaimed that the flower didn't have any smell. "Aren't flowers suppose to smell pretty?" she asked. I answered that some flowers have no smell; they have another gift for us instead. Just like people are different, flowers are all different too.

We continued with our activity until it was time for the closing prayer. I had something special planned. The flower was going to be our sacrifice flower. I had heard this story years ago from Sister José Hobday. It is about a young girl who asked her grandfather how he knew God heard prayers. The grandfather told her to go out to the field and pick any flower she wanted and to bring it back into the house. She proceeded to do so and came back in expecting to find a vase ready for her flower. Instead her grandfather had a special cloth that was laid out in the center of the kitchen table. He told her that God hears prayers; we just don't see it happen. He laid the flower on the cloth and said, "This flower will be our way of knowing that God hears prayers. Each day you can offer your prayers in front of the flower and each day the flower will die a little bit more. As the flower gives up its life, your prayers will be heard by God." Each day the little girl did this, and at the end of a week the flower was all withered up and brown. It had given its life. She and her grandfather went out to the yard and he told her to choose a spot where they could place the dead flower in the soil. She buried the flower as her grandfather said a prayer for life. The next spring she noticed that flowers, just like the one that she had picked, were growing where she had buried the dead one.

After telling the story, I told the children that the flower was to be our sacrifice flower like the one in the story. I had a special cloth and laid it on the table. Then I removed the flower from the water and laid it upon the cloth. We all stood in a circle around the flower and said a prayer. The next week, I again had the flower there as the children entered. Each of them was curious as to how the flower was doing and came close to see. Each week we talked about our prayers and how the flower was showing us that God was hearing our prayers by giving up its life. At the end of the final session we all went outside to an area I had found where we could bury the flower. We circled the area and I let the children take turns digging a hole for the flower. The flower had been carried gently on its cloth with us. My young friend asked if she could place the flower into its spot. She laid it down very gently into the earth and each child was given a turn to sprinkle dirt upon the dead flower. We held hands in our circle and said a blessing for life. The next year a small patch of purple flowers was discovered.

The question is, can we in this process mainstream, or blend, with persons with special needs? I think the answer is yes. If the individual is able IN ANY WAY to be present, to take part in the group or event, to share their thoughts and feelings in creative ways, to express their faith in Jesus, to have a prayer life, to experience a change of heart, then the answer is yes. What this means is that the director/coordinator of the process must meet with those on the team working with the persons with disabilities. In the meeting there will need to be information and material for study by the team members on how to work with and minister to these individuals. When passing on the faith, much of the material we already use can be the same or adapted for those with special needs. There are times when we have not had any previous encounter with a specific disability. We then need to become informed. It is crucial that all on the team are informed and have a clear understanding of the need for an open attitude towards those with disabilities.

Marie Montessori was ahead of her time in education and formational learning. She was a pioneer for those with disabilities and learning challenges. Her main focus was to use the five senses of the person in her teaching. We each experience taste, smell, hearing, sight, and touch. Through these five experiences in our everyday living we learn and respond. When something is seen as beautiful, we may respond by watching in silence or we may speak to its beauty aloud. When bread is cooking in the oven, it fills the air of a home so all can smell and respond with hunger for a taste or just enjoy the smell. If food does not taste good we respond by spitting it out or by making a face of distaste. We also will not order or eat that item again. The senses are usable tools with which to teach. So, Marie did. Jesus taught with everyday life senses too. He used touch for healing and offering compassion, he offered a taste of his life and death with bread and wine, he gave us teachings through the beauty of sight, he heard the cries and needs of others around him. With each of his senses he taught and responded to others.

How can we teach about the Eucharist without some form of bread and wine or grape juice in a chalice on the prayer table? When teaching about Eucharist, using the symbol of a loaf of bread to break at the close of a session is quite meaningful. Have you ever baked bread during a session? This is powerful for all involved. I once decided to make yeast bread during a retreat day with the children. All the ingredients were measured out ahead of time. The twenty children gathered around the area, and we began the process of making bread. Each child had a turn at something, whether pouring, stirring, or kneading. All through the day we would go about other activities while the bread did "its thing." Then we would take breaks and re-gather and say another blessing for the new and different stage the bread was about to go through. At the end of the process we cut the two loaves in slices and each ate it like it was the best in the world.

I cannot encourage you enough to be open to God's work in all people, whoever they are, at whatever age or circumstance. As directors or coordinators, we may think that the people coming are called to learn; however, when we are faced with a challenge, we are the learners. There are times when the process does not lend itself to serving those with specific disabilities. Maybe the group is too large; the location is not convenient, etc. Consequently, there will be a need to adapt the process to fit the spiritual formation for those wanting to learn. Maybe a smaller group in another space, or maybe meeting in a home will serve the needs better. Parents and families are your biggest support team. Ongoing communication with them is necessary. It might be the parents who are involved with you in the formation of their children, or it might be the spouse and children of the adult in the process who are involved.

One young woman called me and asked that she be given the teachings of the church. She had been baptized in another Christian tradition and was determined to become Catholic. I invited her to come and meet me for a conversation to share some additional information. She asked if I ever went out to a person's home. I answered that I hadn't, but I certainly could. We set a date. When the day arrived, I drove to her home and found a beautiful woman in a wheelchair. She was paraplegic and had been in the chair for ten years. Her friend, who had come over to be with her and to listen to what we had to share, welcomed me in. The lady friend was a longtime friend and became her sponsor. Our conversation lasted about an hour. The friend filled out the short form for her. As I remember, she attended two sessions with the group before she became too ill to attend again. She had little stamina. Her friend continued to attend all the sessions. So that she could continue to take part in what was going on in the sessions, I would meet her and her friend to go over the material shared during the sessions she missed. What was profound was the rest of the group. They missed her and would continue to pray for her at each session. Some of them wanted to visit her or write her letters or call and talk. Eventually, three of the group and the friend began to share about the sessions with her, and I was no longer needed at each visit. This was a blessing for all involved. We all grew spiritually and were enriched in faith. The woman was not well enough to celebrate the sacraments with the group at the scheduled date. However, two months later she was able to do so, and the entire group came to celebrate with her. During these experiences it is God who is in control. All we have to do is look around and listen, and we can see God's loving hand at work in all who are present.

CHAPTER EIGHTEEN:

PLANNING SESSIONS IN THE PROCESS

For the catechumenate process we are encouraged to *not* plan. This is because we are to *be* with those who come, *listen* to what they have to share, and then put together an agenda for the next session. This is all well and good, but we also have to be prepared to welcome people and to listen to them. We need to be prepared to guide those who come to share what their interests or issues are, who ask those nagging questions they have always wanted to ask. We need to keep in mind that as we prepare as a team or as facilitators, we are an expression of honesty, trust, and acceptance. We are the examples the participants look to. The following list is a simple guide of those areas, or elements, we as facilitators need to prepare ourselves in so that we can listen and then share as appropriate.

Hospitality: Welcome them at the door, extend a hand of welcome and smile. Will they need a nametag? Do they need to sign in so that you or another team member can contact them for any reason? Will you have beverages or some snack to offer? Are the other team members ready to welcome them too? Is there a comfortable seat ready? Is the room welcoming, or is it a storage space for seasonal parish items? Consider them as guests of the church. Treat them as such.

Welcoming: When everyone has gathered, this is the time of formal welcome. These first words are important to help all present become more comfortable in their environment and with each other. Does our welcome show the importance of each person to the group? Determine which team members have the gift of charisma. Maybe they are extroverts who don't mind being in front of people. What words of welcome can be said to help everyone feel the openness of those facilitating? What opening prayer can be said during this time to help provide a place of acceptance?

Acceptance: It is important to get to know everyone by first name. This can be done simply with a facilitator leading. An icebreaker can be used which will invite them to share their first names and one thing they want others to know. Because the precatechumenate is about their needs, find out one question they came with that can be answered during that or another session. As the participants attend and share, and the sessions continue, the feeling of being accepted should grow. This is the beginning of the participants' sharing their life stories. One simple beginning question is "Where did you find joy during this last week?" As time goes on, more reflective questions can be asked to develop their stories. Acceptance is not achieved in one session; it happens over time. It is also part of the environment of the session, which includes the surroundings and the people present.

Listening: As everyone continues to gather, and each listens to the others, a bond can begin to develop. As each session continues, and the Scripture chosen for the session is shared with the group, trust can begin to grow. There may also be a beginning recognition that their own stories and the stories of others in the group, along with the Scripture shared, relate to each other. They will hear each others' joys, struggles, and pain, and be able to relate this to Jesus' story.

Teaching: What does the church say about _____? We as catechists do *not* teach our opinions. We teach what the church teaches. If we have questions or issues, then we figure out the appropriate response on our own time, not in one of these sessions. We need to remember to teach coming from the participant's life experience, relate it to the events of Jesus' life, and then to how we as church live this out. As this is presented, they will see the challenges they face, what challenges the church faces, where things are right in their life, and where changes need to be made. They will begin the journey to conversion even as they still have doubts or questions.

Challenging: When they meet the challenge of being called to change, it is time for prayer and discernment. The practice of prayer and discernment is important for each person's growth on this spiritual journey and it should be introduced early. It will help them focus on what is important and where they are being called. If negative issues surround their journey, prayer and discernment will be very necessary for their strength and endurance to face any changes needed. This will especially show up in the period of the catechumenate.

Sharing: Be prepared when challenges are faced or confronted; there can be an outpouring of emotion or a silence. Either way God is at work in the person. It is important to follow up on either response. When a sponsor is available and the relationship is a good one, then the sharing will be more balanced and vocalized by the individual during the session. This can take place when there is support in those emotional moments of spiritual living. If the relationship with the sponsor is distant or limited, then the facilitator may need to step in and meet with the person, or call to give an opportunity for those conversations that are needed as the journey progresses.

Praying: The practice and teaching of prayer during the precatechumenate begins a support and grounding for the individuals in their faith expression. As they move forward to the catechumenate period, there seems to be a stronger prayer life due to a flowing relationship with God. As the journey continues, their prayer life deepens and strengthens. This is encouraged by the period of purification and enlightenment during the Lenten season, as they ready themselves for the sacraments of initiation. If the prayer life of the individuals is developed well during the entire process, then they will have the relationship they will need for life with God.

Community: A person's prayer life leads them to recognize their need for God and community. We cannot walk this life alone; we need each other. As we face our challenges, begin to change, become more vulnerable for God's work by sharing our own life story with others, we begin to extend ourselves to the larger community. We seek ways of bringing the face of God to others, of sharing the gospel news. This happens by the leaders, team members, sponsors, and the community being an active part in the participants' formation process.

Being Sent: It is initiation that sends us out. We proclaim our belief in public, we declare our love and obedience to God and church, and so we are sent to be disciples of Jesus to the world. Wherever we go, whomever we are with, and for whatever reason we are called, we profess our belief in Christ. As we are sent we share ourselves, we break open our lives for one another. This is the mystery of love that gives us the fire in our hearts to move forward even in torment. Mystagogia is the breaking open of the mysteries in our daily lives. Where did we see Christ and what did we do?

Chapter Nineteen:

Retreats or Days of Reflection for Children and Youth

As you have read, I took part in planning many retreats for the children, youth, and adults in the process. When I began with second grade children who were preparing for the sacraments of reconciliation and first Eucharist, we always provided some kind of retreat experience. I had been on retreats during my Baptist faith formation as a child, then as a teenager and college student. To this day I am still surprised that many parishes do not offer retreats for those preparing for sacraments. An increasing number of parishes do now offer a retreat for the adults, but many do not do the same for children. Some parishes offer a confirmation retreat for the youth and those youth in the catechumenate, but this can defeat some of the purpose, as they may not be receiving the sacraments together, and may not know each other. If the youth group has included the catechumenate youth in some of the sessions, then this may work for them. When the youth and/or children of the catechumenate are split, it is important to consider ahead of time how it may affect the retreat experience for all involved. Just because we have the youth with other youth and children with other children of like ages, this doesn't guarantee the experience will be good for all.

For the catechumenate process, we introduced the retreat experience to the children and youth in the precatechumenate period. This was a first experience for the majority. It was only a day, from 9:00 am to 3:00 pm. It was held in a familiar space on the parish grounds. We decided early on not to take the children and youth off grounds, since many of them were still becoming better acquainted with the parish. Having the retreat at the church provided another way of celebrating church, and gave the children and youth time to build personal connections with the church grounds and with each other in community. I knew they would have other experiences off-grounds for retreats if they continued in our youth programs, so this seemed to benefit all involved. Parents were also happy with this. They knew where their children were, they were able to meet us all for lunch if desired, and it was a way for us as representatives of the church to build trust with the parents as well.

The first retreat for children was during the precatechumenate period. For the majority of the children, usually all of them, the major issues were about trust. This became our focus as we planned the theme and what would take place during the day. The second retreat was for those children and youth preparing to participate in the rite of acceptance into the order of catechumens, which moved them into the catechumenate period. This retreat offered the children and youth further time for discernment on their readiness to move forward, as well as opportunities for reflections on the gospel and the cross.

Activity worksheets with questions are provided to participants during each retreat. These worksheets are collected and read by team members, to help the leader and specific team members know better where the person is in their journey of faith. Reading over some of the material is also helpful to see what message you were able to communicate during the time together. It also can give some understanding of how the person may feel. It is a great way of evaluating your own process.

CHAPTER TWENTY:

ADULT RETREAT OR DAY OF REFLECTION

We held a two-day retreat for the adults once during the catechumenate period of the process. During the precatechumenate we might hold an evening of reflection. Sometimes we had a gathering on a Saturday afternoon with time for reflection, attending Mass together, and sharing a potluck dinner. Each event was planned for the specific group we had, each was custom-made to serve those attending and their needs for growth in the faith. Important to the precatechumenate period is building community and trust. Our focus or theme for our times together was based on these needs. Our goal for any Scripture used, meditation shared, or activity planned was to expand the hearts and minds of the participants by bringing them to confront these needs in their lives of faith. Those in the catechumenate period were farther along in their faith growth. Their retreat would be during the few weeks before Lent. Our team made it clear that all participants were expected to attend this retreat; only those with true hardship issues would be "let off." Those who did not attend were still required to write a letter of discernment and commitment.

Even if the participants or the parish cannot afford a day of reflection or retreat, I encourage every process to have some special activity for those on this journey of faith. When we began, we met on the parish grounds, had sponsors/spouses bring in the dinner for after Mass, and shared a potluck. The day was and still is memorable for all those who attended. As time went by the price we asked for the retreat was literally just that, the cost of a one day retreat, but it was away. If some were unable to afford the expense, the parish helped. What is important is to provide people on this journey with some sacred time away from their everyday distractions.

When a retreat cannot be provided for the adults, an evening or afternoon of reflection can usually be offered instead. This time can be just as beneficial to the participants and give them the time needed to reflect on where they stand in their journey at that moment in their lives. A time of reflection can be as simple or as complex as you have interest in developing. It can be a day from early in the morning to the evening, or part of the day. It depends on the group you are planning for, their situations, and the team you have to help you. If you lack the size team you would like, call on the sponsors to help. They may be present during the entire day or a portion of it, which gives them further interaction with those they are sponsoring.

The following is what was said to those adults discerning to move forward:

Don't allow your head to lead your heart; instead, let your heart drag your mind, even if the mind is fighting.

Moving forward should be done only because you yourself desire it.

Don't move forward for others, for family or friends or marriages, etc.

If, after today, you feel you are not ready, be honest. It is truly wonderful when you can be honest enough with yourself to know that you may not yet be ready—that you may need a little more time to come to a better understanding of what the church and Christ are calling you to.

Now, let's say you decide to remain in inquiry. Does this mean you have failed? No. You have listened to your heart and mind together and discerned with the Holy Spirit that you need more time for growth or nourishment of your faith.

We tend to try to put God in a box; we often spend years studying for our careers, but we want to hurry up our relationship with God. We may not really be growing spiritually if we move too quickly and are surrounded with distractions. The precatechumenate is just the time to do this growing, and if you need more time, it is yours. We need to be comfortable in wherever we are and where we are going.

CHAPTER TWENTY-ONE

REFLECTION TIME FOR CHILDREN AND YOUTH

Although we did not hold overnight retreats with the children and youth, we did hold mini-retreats (daytime) or reflection times during their sessions. It all started with holding a "silent" session with the children and youth one year during the catechumenate period. We explained during the first fifteen minutes what was going to take place, gave time for questions, and then began with prayer. The sessions were only an hour and a half, so the time went quickly and many of them wanted to know when we could do it again! What we forget sometimes is that our society is very noisy; there is sound everywhere we go. To be in silence with only our thoughts, or being guided through silent activities, can make a profound impact on us, no matter how old we are. After we did this once, we began to build it into the year at least twice. These silent sessions were offered at different times of the year, depending on what was happening within the group. The following is one sample of a "silent session."

Child or Youth Silent Reflection Session

Welcome, nametags, and sign-in by parents

Introduction of the silent session:

This session will be in silence starting fifteen minutes from now. If you do have any emergency, please let one of the team know; however, raise your hand or whisper so that the others in our group are not disturbed. The purpose of this silent session is for you to be able to have time for quiet reflection without any distractions. You will be guided through three stations, each asking you for some response about your faith and relationship with God. We will be counted off to form three groups. Each group will stay together and move together. A bell will ring at a certain time to signal you to move to the next station. There will be a team member at each station to address concerns. Remember to raise your hand, speak in whisper; this is a SILENT SESSION.

Share questions or concerns.

Form groups and hand out pencils.

Offer opening prayer.

Station One: Object Table
On a table are many objects, from tennis shoes to water in a bowl, rocks, feathers, shells, a cross, etc. The handout has one question, "Which one of the objects on the table reflects your relationship with God the best? Please explain your answer."

Station Two: Scripture Reading
Form a circle of chairs so that all seated are facing outward. Invite all to be seated. There is a Bible on each chair and a handout is given to each person. Each is invited to look up and read the story of "The Rich Young Man" in Matthew 19:16-22. The handout then has two questions for them to answer. 1. Describe the rich young man's faith in God. 2. What do you feel kept the rich young man from following Jesus?

Station Three: The Story of Father Damien
Each person is given a copy of a shortened version of Fr.

Damien's story to read. Then they are asked to reflect on Fr. Damien's actions and share their thoughts on what he chose to do with his life. This was a free writing station; some wrote a lot and some wrote very little, but everyone wrote something and all were important.

When the final fifteen minutes for stations was up, we had about fifteen more minutes. We asked each person to write one prayer and put it in the "God Box" (Prayer Box). Then we gathered in a circle and heard from each person some simple sharing of their experience of silence. A closing prayer was offered, and parents were at the door ready to take their children home.

Chapter Twenty-Two:

Working with Authority and Sometimes Politics in the Church

There is no spiritual story or endeavor that can be told without sharing some challenges from those in authority in the church. I do believe that if authority in the church, even at the parish level, challenges this process and its meaning for the whole church, it is truly "they" who are being challenged. It is those in this process at the breakthrough of conversion, the earthy, muddy, unclear living, messiness of life level, who really can answer the questions and doubts of the authority. These people are the teams and participants who journey. They can answer whether the process is of value. I reminded the team I worked with that if we were able to reach one person it was a blessing. When working with the process, we move slowly. When working with authority it can be even slower. The process itself brings change, which is transition, which can be viewed by some as chaos. Until we are able to get it right, we will keep trying. But, we do need to pay attention to how we are trying and what we are trying with! Is it with the knowledge and understanding of the rite? Are we forming others alongside ourselves to aid in the process? Are the staff and priests of the parish part of the formation?

Some of the questions and challenges that my husband and I have had to work with have been:

1. How can children of young age really know they are ready to receive the sacraments?

2. What signs are apparent in the readiness of the

children to show they are ready, and have a clear understanding, for receiving the sacraments of baptism, confirmation, and Eucharist?

3. How can any child really grasp the depth and meaning of all three sacraments of initiation at one time?

4. Why place those children who are candidates, already baptized in the Catholic tradition, into a group with others who are not baptized yet? Shouldn't they go into classes for regular catechism?

5. If we place the child candidate (already baptized) with the child inquirer (unbaptized), are we in fact disrespecting the sacrament of baptism?

6. Priest comment: "I will not confirm any child younger than teenage. There is no way they can understand the commitment of the sacrament."

7. Priest comment: "This adult is already baptized in another Christian tradition and they have a clear understanding of Scripture. They have been well indoctrinated and have great knowledge. I don't think they need the full process of the catechumenate. I have told them they will complete initiation this Easter."

8. Parent comment: "My child is seven years old and not yet baptized. I would like her to receive baptism so that she can receive first communion with her class in school. Your pastor said I needed to see you."

9. Community member comment: "The Easter Vigil is too long for the children; they get too tired and bored to be part of such a night. They need their own celebration."

10. Team member comment: "The scrutinies are too sad and serious for children to understand, they need to experience a different kind of rite or ritual for their age."

11. Why does preparation for sacraments take such a long process for any age?

12. Why is it important to give any other formation than that for the sacraments to those seeking initiation into the church?

These are just some of the most important challenges we have experienced through the years. There were others, and I am certain that you have experienced many. As you read over each question or statement, I hope that what has been written previously gives some insight. We all have questions or concerns with authority these days. In the church it is no different. We know that it is the human element that has been called to lead, and yet we as the church offer our obedience and trust. This is a lot to ask from us these days with the world news as it is. There are a lot of untrustworthy people in any arena of life, even the church. However, it is Jesus who continues to call us, his flock, to listen to him, to hear his voice instead of all others, and to follow. So, we trust what the Holy Spirit is doing within this world. This does not mean that we put on blinders. What it means is that we put on "Jesus eyes." When you put on his glasses, his eyes, you see differently; however, you will see what is real. You see the truth in the beauty and ugliness of life. Are we ready to see and make changes?

I think of Mother Teresa and her eyesight. She had "Jesus eyes." She was able to see the truth before her that was present in each person, their pain and loneliness, lack of hope and spirit. Yet, she did not give in to what the world saw. Her heart chose to see the person dressed in the beauty of life, and although suffering, still hungering for unconditional love. It was this eyesight she reflected to each person seeking her eyes, so that each received the dignity to live and then die in her arms.

It is the eyesight of the whole church that needs to see as Jesus, with his eyes. We need to see each person who comes seeking, for whatever reason, as one who may be suffering and wanting to know they are not alone, lonely and desiring companionship, empty and desiring to be filled, with a story to be told and heard, with gifts to be shared, with knowledge of life to be offered, and as someone longing to touch the robe of Christ. Let the church respond with open arms, ears to listen, hearts filled with compassion, shoulders to bear the pain and burdens, and continue to walk the talk of Jesus. As my husband points out, we are gently placing our lives into the womb of Mother Church. We are not afraid.

Works Cited

International Commission on English in the Liturgy (ICEL) and Bishops' Committee on the Liturgy, *Rite of Christian Initiation for Adults: Study Edition*. Chicago: Liturgy Training Publications, 1988.

Morris, Thomas H. *The RCIA: Transforming the Church*. New York: Paulist Press, 1989.

Oakham, Ron. "Sorting Fish: A Task at the Beginning." *Catechumenate: A Journal of Christian Initiation* II, no 3 (May 1989): 13-19.

Wagner, Nick. *The Way of Faith: A Field Guide for the RCIA Process*. New London, CT: Twenty-third Publications, 2009.

Websters New World Dictionary of the American Language (College Edition). New York: The World Publishing Company, 1979.